Spelling 4
Student Guide

About K12 Inc.

K12 Inc., a technology-based education company, is the nation's leading provider of proprietary curriculum and online education programs to students in grades K–12. K¹² provides its curriculum and academic services to online schools, traditional classrooms, blended school programs, and directly to families. K12 Inc. also operates the K¹² International Academy, an accredited, diploma-granting online private school serving students worldwide. K¹²'s mission is to provide any child the curriculum and tools to maximize success in life, regardless of geographic, financial, or demographic circumstances. K12 Inc. is accredited by CITA. More information can be found at www.K12.com.

Table of Contents

Name _____   Date _____

Unit 1 Spelling List

Words that Follow the Rules

system	(sys-tem)
object	(ob-ject)
admit	(ad-mit)
subject	(sub-ject)
witness	(wit-ness)
insect	(in-sect)
planet	(plan-et)
establishment	(es-tab-lish-ment)
album	(al-bum)
optimist	(op-ti-mist)

Words with Prefixes: The prefix *re-* means again.

renew	(re + new)	(re-new)
replace	(re + place)	(re-place)
reenter	(re + enter)	(re-enter)
review	(re + view)	(re-view)

Related Words

magnet	(magnet)	(mag-net)
magnetize	(magnet + ize)	(mag-net-ize)
magnetic	(magnet + ic)	(mag-net-ic)
magnetism	(magnet + ism)	(mag-net-ism)

Spelling Dangers

people	(peo-ple)
could	(could)

Proper Nouns

Connecticut	(Con-nect-i-cut)
Wisconsin	(Wis-con-sin)

Name _____   Date _____

Get to Know the States
Connecticut and Wisconsin

Use the State Facts pages to complete Parts 1 and 2.

Part 1
Write the name of the state next to its capital.

CAPITAL	STATE
1. Hartford	_____
2. Madison	_____

Part 2
Write a sentence for each state that includes one fact about the state.
Be sure to include the name of the state in your sentence.

For example: The state flower of Iowa is the wild rose.

1._____

_____

2._____

_____

Bonus:
Locate Connecticut and Wisconsin on a map of the United States. Name the state directly to the south of each.

_____ is south of _____.

_____ is south of _____.

State Facts

State	Capital	State Flower	State Bird
Alabama	Montgomery	camellia	yellowhammer
Alaska	Juneau	forget-me-not	willow ptarmigan
Arizona	Phoenix	saguaro blossom	cactus wren
Arkansas	Little Rock	apple blossom	mockingbird
California	Sacramento	California poppy	California valley quail
Colorado	Denver	Rocky Mountain columbine	lark bunting
Connecticut	Hartford	mountain laurel	robin
Delaware	Dover	peach blossom	blue hen chicken
Florida	Tallahassee	orange blossom	mockingbird
Georgia	Atlanta	Cherokee rose	brown thrasher
Hawaii	Honolulu	pua aloalo (yellow hibiscus)	nene
Idaho	Boise	syringa (mock orange)	mountain bluebird
Illinois	Springfield	native violet	cardinal
Indiana	Indianapolis	peony	cardinal
Iowa	Des Moines	wild rose	eastern goldfinch
Kansas	Topeka	sunflower	western meadowlark
Kentucky	Frankfort	goldenrod	cardinal

State Facts

State	Capital	State Flower	State Bird
Louisiana	Baton Rouge	magnolia	eastern brown pelican
Maine	Augusta	pine cone and tassel	chickadee
Maryland	Annapolis	black-eyed Susan	Baltimore oriole
Massachusetts	Boston	Mayflower (trailing arbutus)	chickadee
Michigan	Lansing	apple blossom	robin
Minnesota	St. Paul	(pink and white) lady's slipper	common loon
Mississippi	Jackson	magnolia	mockingbird
Missouri	Jefferson City	hawthorn	bluebird
Montana	Helena	bitterroot	western meadowlark
Nebraska	Lincoln	goldenrod	western meadowlark
Nevada	Carson City	sagebrush	mountain bluebird
New Hampshire	Concord	purple lilac	purple finch
New Jersey	Trenton	purple violet	eastern goldfinch
New Mexico	Santa Fe	yucca	roadrunner
New York	Albany	rose	bluebird
North Carolina	Raleigh	American dogwood	cardinal

State Facts

State	Capital	State Flower	State Bird
North Dakota	Bismarck	wild prairie rose	western meadowlark
Ohio	Columbus	scarlet carnation	cardinal
Oklahoma	Oklahoma City	mistletoe	scissor-tailed flycatcher
Oregon	Salem	Oregon grape	western meadowlark
Pennsylvania	Harrisburg	mountain laurel	ruffed grouse
Rhode Island	Providence	violet	Rhode Island red
South Carolina	Columbia	yellow jessamine	great Carolina wren
South Dakota	Pierre	Pasque	ring-necked pheasant
Tennessee	Nashville	iris	mockingbird
Texas	Austin	bluebonnet	mockingbird
Utah	Salt Lake City	sego lily	California seagull
Vermont	Montpelier	red clover	hermit thrush
Virginia	Richmond	American dogwood	cardinal
Washington	Olympia	rhododendron	willow goldfinch
West Virginia	Charleston	rhododendron	cardinal
Wisconsin	Madison	wood violet	robin
Wyoming	Cheyenne	Indian paintbrush	western meadowlark

Name _____   Date _____

Match the Meaning

Find the spelling words that match the meanings for 1–11. Answer the questions on the next page.

1. To make something fresh again or to start again _____

2. To permit to enter _____

3. A person who gives evidence in court _____

4. To look at or study again _____

5. Humans _____

6. A book in which something is collected _____

7. To go into again _____

8. A business firm _____

9. A person who looks on the bright side _____

10. A piece of iron or steel that can attract iron _____

11. To place again or to take the place of _____

Match the Meaning

12. Find the four meanings on the first page that contain the word *again* and write the spelling words on the lines below.

    _____   _____

    _____   _____

13. What part of each of these words means "again"? _____

14. Write the base word for each of the words in number 12.

    _____   _____

    _____   _____

15. One of the first five answers can also mean "to see something happen."

    What is the word? _____

16. One of the first 11 answers can also mean "a person or thing that puts out a powerful attraction." What is the word? _____

17. Add each of the endings below to the answer in number 16 to create a new word:

    -ize   _____

    -ic   _____

    -ism   _____

Name _____   Date _____

Syllable Match

Read each of the syllables. (They will sound like silly words with no meaning.) Put the syllables together to make one of the spelling words and write the word on a numbered line. After you write the word, write a sentence using the word. The sentence must be at least eight words long. You may make the spelling word plural by adding an *s*. Use each syllable only once.

Syllable List

tem   ob   sect   plan   sys   ject   in   et

1. _____

   _____

2. _____

   _____

3. _____

   _____

4. _____

   _____

Name _____ Date _____

Number Words

Write the name for each number below, then have someone check your work.

If you misspell any words, look in the dictionary for the correct spelling, draw a line through the word you spelled incorrectly and write the correct spelling. Have your spelling checked again.

10 _____

20 _____

30 _____

40 _____

50 _____

60 _____

70 _____

80 _____

90 _____

Name _____ Date _____

Unit 2 Spelling List

Words that Follow the Rules

standing	(stand-ing)
blender	(blend-er)
smashed	(smashed)
spilling	(spill-ing)
sticker	(stick-er)
fixing	(fix-ing)
stepped	(stepped)
splitting	(split-ting)
jammed	(jammed)
thinner	(thin-ner)

Words with Prefixes: The prefix *un-* means *not*.

uncommon	(un + common)	(un-com-mon)
unaware	(un + aware)	(un-a-ware)
unbroken	(un + broken)	(un-bro-ken)
unknown	(un + known)	(un-known)

Related Words

create	(create)	(cre-ate)
creativity	(create - e + ivity)	(cre-a-tiv-i-ty)
creator	(creat - e + or)	(cre-a-tor)
creation	(create - e + ion)	(cre-a-tion)

Spelling Dangers

sentence	(sen-tence)
through	(through)

Proper Nouns

Kansas	(Kan-sas)
Ohio	(O-hi-o)

Name _____   Date _____

Get to Know the States
Kansas and Ohio

Use the State Facts pages to complete Parts 1 and 2.

Part 1
Write the name of the state next to its capital.

   CAPITAL   STATE

   1. Columbus   _____

   2. Topeka   _____

Part 2
Write a sentence for each state that includes one fact about the state.
Be sure to include the name of the state in your sentence.

For example: The state flower of Iowa is the wild rose.

1._____

   _____

2._____

   _____

Bonus:
Locate Ohio and Kansas on a map of the United States. Name the state directly to the east of each.

_____ is east of _____.

_____ is east of _____.

_____

Name _____ Date _____

Word Meanings

Part 1: Find the spelling word that means the same as the words in parentheses. Write the word on the line provided.

1. Snow in Florida is (not usual). _____

2. Mark is full of (the ability to make things up) _____

   and, with his wild imagination, he often writes

   funny stories.

3. Margaret and Tom were (without the knowledge) _____

   that the circus was coming to town.

4. My (thing I made) for art class is a mobile with _____

   colorful birds.

5. The dog ran (from one end to the other) the _____

   neighbor's yard when he was chasing the cat.

6. A (group of words that expresses a complete _____

   thought) begins with a capital letter and ends

   with a period, question mark, or

   exclamation point.

Word Meanings

Part 2: Some words can have more than one meaning. Two definitions for three of the spelling words are shown below. Write the spelling word that matches both definitions on the line provided. Make up two sentences for each word: one sentence for each definition.

Hint: You may use a dictionary to look up meanings.

7. Definition one: squeezed into a space
   Definition two: unworkable because a moving part is stuck

   _____

   Your sentences:

   _____

   _____

8. Definition one: a group of words that expresses a complete thought
   Definition two: the punishment given to a person convicted in a criminal trial

   _____

   Your sentences:

   _____

   _____

9. Definition one: enter in one side and go out the other side
   Definition two: finished

   _____

   Your sentences:

   _____

   _____

Name _____   Date _____

Adding Endings

Add the suffix at the top of each column to the base word in the first column. Write the words in the spaces provided. The rules for adding vowel suffixes to one syllable words are listed below and two examples have been completed for you.

- If the word ends in two or more consonants, just add the suffix.
- If the word has one vowel followed by one consonant, double the consonant before adding the suffix. If the consonant is x, just add the suffix.

When you finish filling in the table, answer the questions on the next page.

Hint: Verbs that change their form are provided. The shaded space means there is no such word.

Base word	Suffix		
	-ed	-er	-ing
example: crush	crushed	crusher	crushing
example: dim	dimmed	dimmer	dimming
1. fix			
2. thin			
3. spill			
4. blend			
5. jam			
6. step			
7. smash			
8. stick	stuck		
9. split	split		
10. stand	stood		

Adding Endings

Answer these questions using words from the table:

1. What is a machine used to make icy drinks and, sometimes, to crush ice?

    _____

2. What word might be used to describe what the plumber is doing when he is repairing a dripping sink?

    _____

3. What word describes something that is breaking in two?

    _____

Bonus:
Write the three words from the Spelling List with the suffix -ed.

_____   _____

_____

How many syllables does each word you wrote have? _____

Name _____   Date _____

Unit 3 Spelling List

Words that Follow the Rules

mixes	(mix-es)
buzzes	(buzz-es)
diminishes	(di-min-ish-es)
glasses	(glass-es)
crunches	(crunch-es)
emblems	(em-blems)
recommends	(rec-om-mends)
infants	(in-fants)
connects	(con-nects)
invents	(in-vents)

Words with Prefixes: The prefix *dis-* means opposite or absence of (lack).

disagree	(dis + agree)	(dis-a-gree)
discomfort	(dis + comfort)	(dis-com-fort)
disrespect	(dis + respect)	(dis-re-spect)
disappear	(dis + appear)	(dis-ap-pear)

Related Words

act	(act)	(act)
actor	(act + or)	(ac-tor)
interact	(inter + act)	(in-ter-act)
react	(re + act)	(re-act)

Spelling Dangers

rough	(rough)
enough	(e-nough)

Proper Nouns

Arkansas	(Ar-kan-sas)
New Hampshire	(New Hamp-shire)

Name _____   **Date** _____

Get to Know the States
Arkansas and New Hampshire

Use the State Facts pages to complete Parts 1 and 2.

Part 1
Write the name of the state next to its capital.

CAPITAL	STATE
1. Concord	_____
2. Little Rock	_____

Part 2
Write a sentence for each state that includes one fact about the state.
Be sure to include the name of the state in your sentence.

For example: The state flower of Iowa is the wild rose.

1._____

_____

2._____

_____

Bonus:
Name the state tree for Arkansas and New Hampshire.

The _____ is the state tree of _____.

The _____ is the state tree of _____.

Name _____ Date _____

Crossword Fun

Use words from the Spelling List to solve the puzzle.

Crossword Fun

Across

2.   to go out of sight

5.   a person who plays a part in a movie or play

7.   to do or behave

8.   having an uneven or irregular surface

10.   the sounds bees make

12.   to talk or do things with other people

13.   very young babies

15.   symbols

17.   lenses used to improve one's eyesight

18.   to act in response to something

19.   makes up something new

Down

1.   as much or many as necessary

2.   the opposite of comfort

3.   gives a good review

4.   state capital is Little Rock

6.   joins two things together

9.   lessens or gets smaller

11.   to be rude to someone

14.   to have a different opinion

16.   blends together

Name _____   Date _____

Opposites

Fix the following sentences by replacing the underlined word or words with a word from the Spelling List that has the opposite meaning. Write the spelling word on the line provided.

1. My sister <u>separates</u> fruit and milk to make a healthy drink.   _____

2. Tom <u>copies</u> stories for his writing assignments.   _____

3. The <u>adults</u> were so cute when they learned to crawl.   _____

4. I <u>think very highly of</u> people who tell lies.   _____

5. Three scoops was <u>too little</u> ice cream for dessert.   _____

6. The movie is so good that my sister <u>gives a bad review to</u> it.   _____

7. The size of a snowman <u>increases</u> as the sun melts it.   _____

8. The water was so <u>smooth</u> when we went sailing that all of us got seasick.   _____

9. In my friend's magic show, he makes a dove <u>show up</u> behind a scarf.   _____

10. Wearing shoes that were too small caused me much <u>ease and enjoyment</u>.   _____

11. When everyone at the meeting starts talking at the same time, the room <u>is completely quiet</u>.   _____

Opposites

12. In her science experiment, Beth <u>pulls apart</u> two wires to make an electric circuit.

    _____

13. The sisters always <u>think alike</u> and want to listen to different music.

    _____

14. How did the man <u>not pay any attention</u> when he was told that he was the winner?

    _____

Name _____   Date _____

Unit 4 Spelling List

Words that Follow the Rules

fragrant	(fra-grant)
danger	(dan-ger)
bacon	(ba-con)
waiting	(wait-ing)
sustain	(sus-tain)
layer	(lay-er)
essay	(es-say)
erase	(e-rase)
exhale	(ex-hale)
scale	(scale)

Words with Prefixes: The prefix *pre-* means before.

prehistoric	(pre + history - y + ic)	(pre-his-tor-ic)
precaution	(pre + caution)	(pre-cau-tion)
prefix	(pre + fix)	(pre-fix)
preview	(pre + view)	(pre-view)

Related Words

export	(ex + port)	(ex-port)
import	(im + port)	(im-port)
transport	(trans + port)	(trans-port)
portable	(port + able)	(port-a-ble)

Spelling Dangers

though	(though)
although	(al-though)

Proper Nouns

Mississippi	(Mis-sis-sip-pi)
Maine	(Maine)

Name _____   Date _____

Get to Know the States
Mississippi and Maine

Use the State Facts pages to complete Parts 1 and 2.

Part 1
Write the name of the state next to its capital.

CAPITAL   STATE

1. Jackson   _____

2. Augusta   _____

Part 2
Write a sentence for each state that includes one fact about the state.
Be sure to include the name of the state in your sentence.

For example: The state flower of Iowa is the wild rose.

1._____

_____

2._____

_____

Bonus:
Locate Mississippi and Maine on a map of the United States. Name the state or states directly to the west of each

_____ is west of _____.

_____ are west of _____ .

_____

Name _____   Date _____

Word Sort

Part 1: Sort the words in the Spelling List with the long *a* sound according to their spelling of the sound.

a	ai	ay	a-consonant-e

Part 2: Find all the words in the Spelling List with a prefix or suffix. Write each word on the lines below. One syllable has already been provided for each word. When you have filled in all the words, circle all prefixes and suffixes.

1. _____ ing

2. _____ er

3. _____ hale

4. pre _____ ic

5. _____ caution

6. pre _____

7. _____ view

8. ex _____

9. im _____

10. trans _____

11. port _____

Word Sort

Part 3: Write the words from Part 2 in alphabetical order.

Hint: You will have to look at the fourth letter in the words with the prefix pre- when deciding how to alphabetize.

1. _____

2. _____

3. _____

4. _____

5. _____

6. _____

7. _____

8. _____

9. _____

10. _____

11. _____

Name _____   Date _____

Writing Definitions

Select three words from the list below and write your own definition for each. Tell whether the word is a noun or a verb. Use the word in a sentence, making sure the meaning of the word in your sentence matches the definition. An example is shown.

Hint: You may use the dictionary to look up any definition.

erase   bacon   sustain   scale   prefix   preview

Example: exhale – verb – to breathe out
When we exhale, our body gets rid of carbon dioxide.

1. word: _____ noun or verb? _____

   definition: _____

   _____

   my sentence: _____

   _____

2. word: _____ noun or verb? _____

   definition: _____

   _____

   my sentence: _____

Writing Definitions

3. word: _____ noun or verb? _____

   definition: _____

   _____

   my sentence: _____

   _____

Name _____ Date _____

Unit 5 Spelling List

Words that Follow the Rules

weightless	(weight-less)
eighteen	(eigh-teen)
neighborly	(neigh-bor-ly)
weighing	(weigh-ing)
freighter	(freight-er)
obey	(o-bey)
survey	(sur-vey)
convey	(con-vey)
daybreak	(day-break)
steakhouse	(steak-house)

Words with Prefixes: The prefix *sub-* means under.

substandard	(sub + standard)	(sub-stand-ard)
submarine	(sub + marine)	(sub-ma-rine)
subtitle	(sub + title)	(sub-ti-tle)
subway	(sub + way)	(sub-way)

Related Words

flex	(flex)	(flex)
flexible	(flex + ible)	(flex-i-ble)
inflexible	(in + flex + ible)	(in-flex-i-ble)
reflex	(re + flex)	(re-flex)

Spelling Dangers

bought	(bought)
thought	(thought)

Proper Nouns

Pennsylvania	(Penn-syl-va-nia)
Texas	(Tex-as)

Name _____   Date _____

Get to Know the States
Pennsylvania and Texas

Use the State Facts pages to complete Parts 1 and 2.

Part 1
Write the name of the state next to its capital.

CAPITAL   STATE

1. Austin   _____

2. Harrisburg   _____

Part 2
Write a sentence for each state that includes one fact about the state.
Be sure to include the name of the state in your sentence.

For example: The state flower of Iowa is the wild rose.

1. _____

   _____

2. _____

   _____

Bonus:
Name the state mottoes for Pennsylvania and Texas.

_____ is the state

motto of _____.

_____ is the state motto of _____.

_____

Name _____   Date _____

How Good Is Your Memory?

Try to remember the spelling word that fits the clue. If you can remember the word, write it on the first line after the clue. If you have to look at the Spelling List, write the word on the second line. When you have finished, count the answers you remembered and spelled correctly, then count the answers you spelled correctly after you looked at the Spelling List. Record your score at the bottom of the page.

	I remember the word	I looked for the word
1. This word means underwater.	_____	_____
2. This is what you do when you look something over.	_____	_____
3. This describes something that is not able to bend.	_____	_____
4. This is another word for sunrise.	_____	_____
5. You would find this written under a title.	_____	_____
6. This is the number of items you would have if you had 2 less than 20.	_____	_____
7. You can ride on a train in this underground passage.	_____	_____
8. This is a large ship that carries cargo.	_____	_____
9. This means to follow instructions.	_____	_____
10. Someone who is kind and friendly is said to act this way.	_____	_____

Number of correct answers I remembered: _____

_____

Name _____

Date _____

Word Sort

Part 1: Sort the words in the Spelling List with a long *a* sound, according to their spelling of the sound.

eigh	ey	ea	ay	a

Part 2: Find all the words in the Spelling List with a prefix or suffix. Write each base word on the correct line below. The prefixes and suffixes have already been provided.

example: eight _____ een

1. sub _____

2. _____ ing

3. _____ ible

4. sub _____

5. _____ er

6. _____ less

7. sub _____

8. re _____

9. sub _____

10. _____ ly

11. in _____ ible

Name _____   Date _____

Unit 6 Spelling List

Words that Review Spelling Rules

absent	(ab-sent)
habitat	(hab-i-tat)
skimmed	(skimmed)
cashed	(cashed)
sandboxes	(sand-box-es)
contests	(con-tests)
afraid	(a-fraid)
major	(ma-jor)
eighty	(eight-y)
breaking	(break-ing)

Words that Review Prefixes

disapprove	(dis + approve)	(dis-ap-prove)
preorder	(pre + order)	(pre-or-der)
reproduce	(re + produce)	(re-pro-duce)
unlucky	(un + lucky)	(un-luck-y)

Words that Review Related Words

creating	(create - e + ing)	(cre-at-ing)
magnets	(magnet + s)	(mag-nets)
action	(act + ion)	(ac-tion)
transporting	(transport + ing)	(trans-port-ing)

Name _____   Date _____

Get to Know the States Review

Write the name of the state next to its state capital.

Hint: You may use the State Facts pages.

CAPITAL	STATE
1. Austin	_____
2. Little Rock	_____
3. Topeka	_____
4. Madison	_____
5. Harrisburg	_____
6. Columbus	_____
7. Concord	_____
8. Jackson	_____
9. Hartford	_____
10. Augusta	_____

Bonus:
Write the two-letter postal abbreviation after each state name.
For example: New York NY

Name _____ Date _____

Base Words

Part 1: Eight words in the Spelling List have the suffixes *-s, -es, -ed,* or *-ing.* Write each of these words next to its definition and circle the suffix.

1. carrying from one place to another _____

2. several pieces of iron that attract other pieces of iron _____

3. making or designing _____

4. falling into pieces _____

5. more than one race _____

6. boxes that hold sand for children to play in _____

7. moved lightly and quickly over a surface _____

8. received dollar bills for a check _____

Part 2: Find the word in the Spelling List with a base word that matches each definition. Write the spelling word on the line next to the definition and underline the base word. Circle the prefix and draw a line to its meaning. The first one has been done for you.

1. having good fortune   (un)lucky   a. again

2. to make something _____ b. not

3. to request a supply of goods _____ c. opposite of

4. to say something is good or suitable _____ d. before

Name _____   Date _____

Spelling Dangers

Find the words in the Spelling Dangers Word Bank that have the sounds listed. Remember that you are looking for the same sounds, not the same spellings. Write the words on the line or lines after the sound.

Spelling Dangers Word Bank

bought	rough	through	could	sentence
people	thought	although	enough	though

1. /ē/ as in s*ee*   _____

2. /ō/ as in n*o*   _____   _____

3. /o͞o/ as in sch*oo*l   _____

4. /aw/ as in cl*aw*   _____   _____

5. /s/ as in *s*ip   _____

6. /f/ as in i*f*   _____   _____

7. /k/ as in *k*ite   _____

Name _____   Date _____

Questions and Prefixes

Part 1: Find words from the Spelling List to answer the questions. Write the answers on the lines.

1. Which word is a compound word? (A compound word is two words joined to make one word.)

    _____

2. Which word has the final consonant in the base word doubled before adding

    the suffix? _____

3. Which word is a number? _____

4. Which word has a prefix meaning "before"? _____

5. Which word has a prefix meaning "not"?_____

6. Which word has a prefix meaning "the opposite of"? _____

7. Which word has a base word meaning "to act"? _____

8. Which word rhymes with pager? _____

9. How is the /er/ sound spelled in the word that answers #8?

    _____

10. Write all the words with one syllable. _____

    _____

Questions and Prefixes

Part 2: Insert the prefix that best completes the italicized word in each sentence.

re- means again   *pre-* means before   *sub-* means under   *un-* means not

dis- means opposite or absence of (lack)

1. The store had a _____ *season* sale of winter coats in August.

2. I lost her address so I am _____ *sure* as to which house is hers.

3. The roots of flowers don't usually grow very deep, but tree roots reach deep

   down into the_____ *soil.*

4. I had to_____*write* the list after I lost the first copy.

5. Sometimes my brother and I _____*agree* about which game
   to play.

Name _____   Date _____

Unit 7 Spelling List

Words that Follow the Rules

reduce	(re-duce)
remain	(re-main)
determine	(de-ter-mine)
plead	(plead)
breathe	(breathe)
eager	(ea-ger)
freedom	(free-dom)
chimpanzee	(chim-pan-zee)
extreme	(ex-treme)
evening	(eve-ning)

Words with Prefixes: The prefix _dis-_ means not, to do the opposite.

disarm	(dis + arm)	(dis-arm)
dishonest	(dis + honest)	(dis-hon-est)
disregard	(dis + regard)	(dis-re-gard)
disable	(dis + able)	(dis-a-ble)

Related Words

structure	(struct + ure)	(struc-ture)
construction	(con + struct + ion)	(con-struc-tion)
instruct	(in + struct)	(in-struct)
obstruction	(ob + struct + ion)	(ob-struc-tion)

Spelling Dangers

answer	(an-swer)
listen	(lis-ten)

Proper Nouns

Tennessee	(Ten-nes-see)
Alabama	(Al-a-bam-a)

Name _____ Date _____

Get to Know the States
Tennessee and Alabama

Use the State Facts pages to complete Parts 1 and 2.

Part 1
Write the name of the state next to its capital.

CAPITAL   STATE

1. Nashville   _____

2. Montgomery   _____

Part 2
Write a sentence for each state that includes one fact about the state. Be sure to include the name of the state in your sentence.

1. _____

   _____

2. _____

   _____

Bonus: Name the state trees for Tennessee and Alabama.

The state tree of _____ is the _____ .

The state tree of _____ is the _____ .

Name _____ Date _____

Word Sort

Part 1
Sort the words in the Spelling List according to their spelling of the long *e* sound.

e	ee	ea	*e*-consonant-*e*

Part 2
Use words from the table to complete the definitions.

1. To take air into the lungs and let it out means to _____.

2. To ask in a serious way means to _____.

3. To make smaller or decrease means to _____.

4. To find something out exactly means to _____.

5. To stay behind while others go means to _____.

Name _____   **Date** _____

Prefix Practice and Root Review

Part 1:
Add the prefix *dis-* to each of the words and write them on the lines. Select two of the new words you have created and write a sentence for each.

Hint: The prefix *dis-* means not, or the opposite of.

1. agree _____   5. please _____

2. obey _____   6. honor _____

3. appear _____   7. trust _____

4. honest _____   8. like _____

Word	Sentence

Part 2:

Use one of the Related Words to complete each sentence. If you wish, illustrate one of the sentences on the back of this page.

Hint: The root *struct* means build.

1. _____ workers wear hard hats for safety.

2. The wisest of the three pigs lived in a brick _____.

3. The fallen tree was an _____ in the road.

4. Our Girl Scout leader will _____ the troop about

camping.

Name _____   Date _____

Editing Sentences

There is a misspelled word in each of the following sentences. Underline the misspelled word and write the correct spelling on the line.

1. Nashville is the capital of Tennassee. _____

2. Only two tasks remane on my list of "things to do". _____

3. I had to pleed with Dad to let me go to the beach. _____

4. Last evning our pet cat stayed outside all night. _____

5. When we saw the picture of the vacation resort, we were eger to pack

    our bags. _____

6. Mom asked me to anser the door. _____

7. If we always tell the truth, we will never be dishonist.

    _____

8. In the winter, we sometimes have xtreme weather. _____

9. I need help to determin which basketball shoes are best to buy.

    _____

10. We must reduse the use of our natural resources. _____

Name _____   Date _____

Unit 8 Spelling List

Words that Follow the Rules

greedy	(greed-y)
fantasy	(fan-ta-sy)
agency	(a-gen-cy)
chimney	(chim-ney)
attorney	(at-tor-ney)
thief	(thief)
achieve	(a-chieve)
believe	(be-lieve)
receive	(re-ceive)
ceiling	(ceil-ing)

Words with Prefixes: The prefix *en-* means to make or cause to be.

enjoy	(en + joy)	(en-joy)
endanger	(en + danger)	(en-dan-ger)
enrich	(en + rich)	(en-rich)
entangle	(en + tangle)	(en-tan-gle)

Related Words

scribe	(scrib + e)	(scribe)
scribble	(scrib + ble)	(scrib-ble)
describe	(de + scrib + e)	(de-scribe)
prescribe	(pre + scrib + e)	(pre-scribe)

Spelling Dangers

calendar	(cal-en-dar)
grammar	(gram-mar)

Proper Nouns

New Jersey	(New Jer-sey)
Kentucky	(Ken-tuck-y)

Name _____   Date _____

Get to Know the States
New Jersey and Kentucky

Use the State Facts pages to complete Parts 1 and 2.

Part 1
Write the name of the state next to its capital.

CAPITAL   STATE

   1. Trenton   _____

   2. Frankfort   _____

Part 2
Write a sentence for each state that includes one fact about the state. Be sure to include the name of the state in your sentence.

1. _____

   _____

2. _____

   _____

Bonus:
Name the United States presidents who were born in Kentucky and New Jersey.

_____ was born in _____.

_____ was born in _____.

Name William   Date 11/15/17

Mystery Letters

Circle the correct letter or letters to complete each word. Write the word on the line. Try to complete this exercise without looking at the Spelling List.

1. greed____   e   (y)   greedy

2. c____ling   (ei)   ie   ceiling

3. chimn____   y   (ey)   chimney

4. th____f   (ie)   ei   thief

5. d____scribe   ee   (e)   describe

6. New Jers____   (ey)   y   New Jersey

7. ach____ve   ei   (ie)   achieve

8. pr____scribe   (e)   ee   Prescribe

9. bel____ve   (ie)   ei   believe

10. Kentuck____   (ey)   y   Kentuckey

Name _____   Date _____

Practice Makes Perfect

Part 1: Complete each sentence with a word from the Spelling List.

1. If the forest fire spreads, it will _en_____ the bears' habitat.

2. The wolf climbed down the _____ of the third little pig's house and ended up in the soup pot.

3. Check your composition to make sure the _____ and punctuation are correct.

4. During the contest, we were allowed to _____ our answers rather than take the time to write neatly.

5. Look for today's date on the _____ .

Part 2: The prefix *en-* means to make or cause to be. Write a word with the prefix *en-* that means the same as each phrase. For example, "to cause to be in danger" is the same as endanger.

1. to cause to be in a rage _____

2. to cause to be in a tangle _____

3. to make larger _____

4. to cause to be in a trap _____

5. to make rich _____

6. to make able _____

7. to make a circle around _____

8. to cause to be in force _____

Name _____ Date _____

Word Sort

1. Sort the words in the Spelling List according to their spelling of the long *e* sound.
2. Tell whether the word is a noun, verb, or adjective.
3. Select two of the words and use each word in a sentence.

y	Part of Speech	*ey*	Part of Speech

e	Part of Speech

ie	Part of Speech	*ei*	Part of Speech

Word	Sentence

Name _____   Date _____

Unit 9 Spelling List

Words that Follow the Rules
tiger	(ti-ger)
license	(li-cense)
identify	(i-den-ti-fy)
dynamite	(dy-na-mite)
analyze	(an-a-lyze)
fright	(fright)
recognize	(rec-og-nize)
apologize	(a-pol-o-gize)
excitement	(ex-cite-ment)
enlighten	(en-light-en)

Words with Prefixes: The prefix *mis-* means opposite, bad, or wrong.
misspell	(mis + spell)	(mis-spell)
misprint	(mis + print)	(mis-print)
misjudge	(mis + judge)	(mis-judge)
misfortune	(mis + fortune)	(mis-for-tune)

Related Words
inspect	(in + spec + t)	(in-spect)
spectacles	(spec + tacles)	(spec-ta-cles)
spectator	(spec + tator)	(spec-ta-tor)
prospect	(pro + spec + t)	(pros-pect)

Spelling Dangers
patient	(pa-tient)
everyone	(eve-ry-one)

Proper Nouns
South Carolina	(South Car-o-li-na)
Rhode Island	(Rhode Is-land)

Name _____   Date _____

Get to Know the States
South Carolina and Rhode Island

Use the State Facts pages to complete Parts 1 and 2.

Part 1
Write the name of the state next to its capital.

CAPITAL   STATE

    1. Columbia

                                    _____

    2. Providence

                                      _____

Part 2
Write a sentence for each state that includes one fact about the state. Be sure to include the name of the state in your sentence.

1. _____

   _____

2. _____

   _____

Bonus: Find the nicknames for South Carolina and Rhode Island.

_____ is the nickname for _____ .

_____ is the nickname for _____ .

Word Sort

Part 1: Sort the words in the Spelling List according to their spelling of the long *i* sound.

Hint: Two of the words will be listed twice.

ī	*i-consonant-e*

y	*igh*

Part 2: Use three of the words in sentences.

Word	Sentence

Name _____   Date _____

Match the Meaning

Part 1: Find the spelling word that means the same as the definitions below.

1. one who watches but does not take part _____

2. to identify _____

3. a powerful explosive _____

4. to say that you are sorry for having done something wrong

   _____

5. to teach _____

6. every person _____

7. a paper showing that someone is permitted by law to do something

   _____

8. a large Asian animal that is a member of the cat family, with a light brown

   coat with black stripes _____

Match the Meaning

Part 2: Choose a word from the Word Bank that matches each definition below.

The prefix *mis-* means opposite, bad, or wrong.

Word Bank

misplace	misprint	mismatch
misspell	misfortune	misjudge

1. to spell incorrectly _____

2. to match badly _____

3. to judge wrongly or incorrectly _____

4. to put in the wrong place _____

5. bad luck or bad fortune _____

6. to make a mistake in printing _____

Name _____   Date _____

Complete the Sentence

Find a spelling word to complete each sentence. Write the word on the line.

1. Please help me _____ these plants.

2. The circus caused great _____ in the town.

3. I will _____ to my friend for not meeting him after the game.

4. In science we will _____ pond water and write our findings in a report.

5. It was their _____ to miss the last bus to the amusement park.

6. The _____ was admitted to the hospital for tests.

7. Sarah was excited about the _____ of a long vacation.

8. He didn't want to _____ the number of cookies he would need to buy, so he counted again.

9. In Greek mythology, the creature Medusa is described as quite a

   _____ .

10. Ben Franklin put halves of two different lenses together to make

    _____ that let him see both near and far.

11. The newspaper _____ stated that "the family lived in the horse" rather than "in the house."

12. Did you _____ the vase carefully to make sure it wasn't broken?

Name _____ Date _____

Unit 10 Spelling List

Words that Follow the Rules

tomorrow	(to-mor-row)
thrown	(thrown)
bowling	(bowl-ing)
growth	(growth)
approach	(ap-proach)
boastful	(boast-ful)
coastal	(coast-al)
throat	(throat)
oboe	(o-boe)
foe	(foe)

Words with Prefixes: The prefix *in-* means not.

inadequate	(in + adequate)	(in-ad-e-quate)
insane	(in + sane)	(in-sane)
incorrect	(in + correct)	(in-cor-rect)
incomplete	(in + complete)	(in-com-plete)

Related Words

value	(val + ue)	(val-ue)
valuable	(val + uable)	(val-u-a-ble)
evaluate	(e + val + uate)	(e-val-u-ate)
valueless	(val + ue + less)	(val-ue-less)

Spelling Dangers

across	(a-cross)
ready	(read-y)

Proper Nouns

New York	(New York)
Nevada	(Ne-va-da)

Name _____ Date _____

Get to Know the States
Nevada and New York

Use the State Facts pages to complete Parts 1 and 2.

Part 1
Write the name of the state next to its capital.

CAPITAL   STATE

1. Carson City   _____

2. Albany   _____

Part 2
Write a sentence for each state that includes one fact about the state. Be sure to include the name of the state in your sentence.

1. _____

   _____

2. _____

   _____

Bonus: Name the official state songs of New York and Nevada.

" _____ " is the official state song of

_____ .

" _____ " is the official state song of

_____ .

Name _____ Date _____

Synonym Search

Find the word in the Spelling List that is a synonym (or has the same meaning) for the underlined word or words in the sentences. Write the synonyms on the lines at the end of the sentences.

1. The <u>enemy</u> invaded the town at night. _____

2. The <u>unfinished</u> task was put aside until the next day. _____

3. The gold medal is <u>precious</u> to the athlete. _____

4. American cities experienced <u>an increase</u> in population due to industrial

   inventions. _____

5. My sister said my answer was <u>wrong</u>. _____

6. The ships slowed down when they were ready to <u>come near</u> the harbor.

   _____

7. The beanbags were <u>tossed</u> back and forth among the children.

   _____

8. People in poor countries often have <u>insufficient</u> supplies of food and water.

   _____

9. Dad said to be <u>prepared</u> to leave for vacation at 9 a.m. _____

10. The skating champions will <u>judge</u> the contestants in the competition.

    _____

Name _____   **Date** _____

Word Sort

Sort the Words that Follow the Rules and the words in the Long *o* Word Bank according to their spelling of long *o*.

Long *o* Word Bank					
scarecrow	sideshow	tiptoe	woe	reproach	moat
goalpost	coach	doe	outgrow	rainbow	hoe
approach	oboe	coastal	throat	bowling	
boastful	thrown	tomorrow	foe	growth	

oa	

ow	

oe	

Name _____   Date _____

Word Meanings

Part 1: Find the spelling word that means the same as the definitions below.

1. a woodwind instrument with a high tone _____

2. without value or worth _____

3. the day after today _____

4. a game played with ten pins and a ball _____

5. on the opposite side _____

6. the passage from the mouth to the lungs and stomach _____

7. full of pride _____

8. worth _____

9. on the land near a shore _____

10. a gradual increase _____

Part 2: The prefix *in-* means not. For example, *inaccurate* means not accurate or not correct. Add the prefix *in-* to the following words and write their new meanings.

Word	Word + Prefix *in-*	Meaning
1. adequate		
2. expensive		
3. sane		
4. correct		
5. complete		
6. active		

Name _____ Date _____

Unit 11 Spelling List

Words that Follow the Rules

global	(glo-bal)
solar	(so-lar)
buffalo	(buf-fa-lo)
soldier	(sol-dier)
blindfold	(blind-fold)
trombone	(trom-bone)
decompose	(de-com-pose)
diagnose	(di-ag-nose)
episode	(ep-i-sode)
telescope	(tel-e-scope)

Words with Prefixes: The prefix *bi-* means two.

bicycle	(bi + cycle)	(bi-cy-cle)
biannual	(bi + annual)	(bi-an-nu-al)
biweekly	(bi + weekly)	(bi-week-ly)
bimonthly	(bi + monthly)	(bi-month-ly)

Related Words

rupture	(rupt + ure)	(rup-ture)
interrupt	(inter + rupt)	(in-ter-rupt)
disrupt	(dis + rupt)	(dis-rupt)
erupt	(e + rupt)	(e-rupt)

Spelling Dangers

league	(league)
tongue	(tongue)

Proper Nouns

Oklahoma	(O-kla-ho-ma)
New Mexico	(New Mex-i-co)

Name _____   Date _____

Get to Know the States
Oklahoma and New Mexico

Use the State Facts pages to complete Parts 1 and 2.

Part 1
Write the name of the state next to its capital.

CAPITAL   STATE

1. Sante Fe   _____

2. Oklahoma City   _____

Part 2
Write a sentence for each state that includes one fact about the state. Be sure to include the name of the state in your sentence.

1. _____

   _____

2. _____

   _____

Bonus: Name one of the major rivers in Oklahoma and New Mexico.

A major river in _____ is the _____ River.

A major river in _____ is the _____ River.

Name _____ Date _____

Word Sort

Sort the words in the Spelling List and the words in the Long o Word Bank according to their spelling of long o.

Hint: Two of the words will be listed twice.

Long o Word Bank

notebook	tone	tiptoe	narrow	toenail
raincoat	towboat	growing	cloak	oboe

o	o-consonant-e

oa	ow	oe

Name _____ Date _____

Complete the Sentence

Part 1: Find a spelling word to complete each sentence. Write the word on the line.

1. Please do not _____ when I am talking on the telephone.

2. There are twenty teams in the football _____ .

3. Was the doctor able to _____ the illness?

4. My brother plays _____ in the town band.

5. Scientists think the volcano is ready to _____ .

6. The word _____ means "wild ox."

7. The storm may _____ our plans to go to the beach.

8. You will need a _____ to cover the player's eyes if you plan to play Pin the Tail on the Donkey.

9. The pizza was so hot that I burned my _____ when I took a bite.

10. This airplane is a _____ transport, which means it travels around the world.

Complete the Sentence

Part 2: The prefix *bi-* means two. Read the words and their definitions, then use the words to complete the sentences.

Word	Meaning
bicycle	a vehicle with two wheels, one behind the other
biannual	an event that happens two times a year
biweekly	an activity that happens every other week
bimonthly	an activity that happens every other month
biplane	an airplane with two sets of wings, one above the other
binoculars	a hand-held instrument for seeing at a distance, that is made up of two small telescopes

1. We make _____ visits to the dentist, in other words we go every six months.

2. Use the _____ to see if you can spot any wildlife in the distance.

3. We receive our paychecks _____ , so we get 26 paychecks a year.

4. When I was little I rode a tricycle, but when I got older I learned to ride a

   _____ .

5. Our club meets _____ , we have six meetings a year.

6. At the air show, we saw an old-fashioned airplane with two sets of wings called a _____ .

Name _____   Date _____

The Missing Links

The vowels in the following words are missing. Try to complete each word without looking at the Spelling List. Then write its meaning on the line. Use the meanings in the Definition Depot.

1. r____pt____r____   _____

2. s____ld____ ____r   _____

3. ____p____s____d____   _____

4. bl____ndf____ld   _____

5. gl____b____l   _____

6. s____l____r   _____

7. t____ng____ ____   _____

8. t____l____sc____p____   _____

9. b____w____ ____kl____   _____

10. d____c____mp____s____   _____

Definition Depot	
every second week	pertaining to the sun
organ used in tasting, eating, and speaking	worldwide
instrument used to look at the stars	part of a story
break	decay
person who serves in the army	covering for the eyes

Name _____   Date _____

Unit 12 Spelling List

Words that Review Spelling Rules

redeem	(re-deem)
underneath	(un-der-neath)
monkey	(mon-key)
gravity	(grav-i-ty)
brief	(brief)
magnify	(mag-ni-fy)
exercise	(ex-er-cise)
motivate	(mo-ti-vate)
remote	(re-mote)
erode	(e-rode)

Words that Review Prefixes

injustice	(in + justice)	(in-jus-tice)
encircle	(en + circle)	(en-cir-cle)
misconduct	(mis + conduct)	(mis-con-duct)
disobey	(dis + obey)	(dis-o-bey)

Words that Review Related Words

interrupting	(inter + rupt + ing)	(in-ter-rupt-ing)
valuables	(val + uables)	(val-u-a-bles)
respect	(re + spec + t)	(re-spect)
subscribe	(sub + scribe)	(sub-scribe)

Name _____   Date _____

Get to Know the States Review

Write the name of the state next to its capital.

CAPITAL	STATE
1. Providence	_____
2. Montgomery	_____
3. Frankfort	_____
4. Carson City	_____
5. Oklahoma City	_____
6. Columbia	_____
7. Nashville	_____
8. Albany	_____
9. Santa Fe	_____
10. Trenton	_____

Bonus:
Write the two-letter postal abbreviation after each state name.
For example: New York NY

Name _____ Date _____

Alphabetical Order and Prefix Practice

Part 1: Alphabetize the words in the first column and place them in order in the second column.

Word List	Alphabetical Order
erode	1.
redeem	2.
underneath	3.
exercise	4.
valuables	5.
subscribe	6.
magnify	7.
gravity	8.
monkey	9.
calendar	10.
brief	11.
interrupting	12.
respect	13.
remote	14.

Alphabetical Order and Prefix Practice

Part 2: Find a word in the Word Bank that answers the question. Write the word or words on the line and circle the prefix.

Word Bank		
subscribe	encircle	injustice
bimonthly	disobey	misconduct

1. Which two words have prefixes that mean "not"?

   _____   _____

2. Which word has a prefix that means "to make or cause to be"?

   _____

3. Which word has a prefix that means "two"? _____

4. Which word has a prefix that means "opposite", "bad", or "wrong"?

   _____

5. Which word has a prefix that means "under"? _____

Name _____   Date _____

Spelling Dangers

Find the words in the Spelling Dangers Word Bank that fit the clues. Write the words on the line or lines after the clues.

Spelling Dangers Word Bank				
every	patient	ready	listen	grammar
tongue	across	calendar	league	answer

1. *ti* sounds like /sh/ _____

2. begins with *a* as in *ago* _____

3. ends in /er/ spelled *ar* _____

    _____

4. ends in the sound of long *e* _____   _____

5. has two silent vowels next to one another _____

    _____

6. has a silent consonant _____

    _____

<u>Name</u>_____ <u>Date</u>_____

Answer the Questions

Find a spelling word to answer each of the questions.

1. Which word is a synonym for beneath? _____

2. Which word means "to wear away"? _____

3. Which word rhymes with "grief"? _____

4. Which word as a noun names a mammal with a long tail, and as a verb

    means to "fool around"? _____

5. Which word means "breaking in on"? _____

6. Which word would you use to describe an out-of-the-way place?

    _____

7. Which word means to "exchange for something of value"?

    _____

8. Which word means "a drill" and also means "to train the body"?

    _____

9. What do the lenses of a microscope do? _____

10. Which word describes "articles of great worth"? _____

11. What word names what a coach will do to get his team to try their

    very best? _____

Answer the Questions

12. What do you do when you sign-up to purchase a magazine or newspaper?

    _____

13. What is the force that pulls objects down to the Earth?

    _____

14. Which word means "to show honor"? _____

Name _____   Date _____

Unit 13 Spelling List

Words that Follow the Rules

pupil	(pu-pil)
community	(com-mu-ni-ty)
uniform	(u-ni-form)
union	(u-nion)
university	(u-ni-ver-si-ty)
argue	(ar-gue)
refugee	(ref-u-gee)
cue	(cue)
commute	(com-mute)
execute	(ex-e-cute)

Words with Prefixes: The prefix *semi-* means half or partly.

semifinal	(semi + final)	(sem-i-fi-nal)
semipro	(semi + pro)	(sem-i-pro)
semicircle	(semi + circle)	(sem-i-cir-cle)
semiskilled	(semi + skilled)	(sem-i-skilled)

Related Words

dictate	(dict + ate)	(dic-tate)
dictator	(dict + ator)	(dic-ta-tor)
dictionary	(dict + ionary)	(dic-tion-ar-y)
predict	(pre + dict)	(pre-dict)

Spelling Dangers

restaurant	(res-tau-rant)
against	(a-gainst)

Proper Nouns

Virginia	(Vir-gin-ia)
Georgia	(Geor-gia)

Name _____   Date _____

Get to Know the States
Virginia and Georgia

Use the State Facts pages to complete Parts 1 and 2.

Part 1: Write the name of the state next to its capital.

	CAPITAL		STATE
1.	Richmond		_____
2.	Atlanta		_____

Part 2: Write a sentence for each state that includes one fact about the state. Be sure to include the name of the state in your sentence.

1. _____

   _____

2. _____

   _____

Bonus: Name the states that are located between Virginia and Georgia.

The states located between _____ and _____

are _____ and _____ .

Name _____   Date _____

Word Sort

Part 1: Sort the Words that Follow the Rules and the words in the Long *u* Word Bank according to their spelling of long *u*.

Long *u* Word Bank				
menu	unit	dispute	avenue	tribute
revenue	January	music	compute	humor

u		

ue	*u-consonant-e*	

Part 2: Select two of the words and use each in a sentence.

Word   **Sentence**

_____   _____

                        _____

_____   _____

                        _____

Name _____   Date _____

Synonym Sandwiches

Put the tops on the synonym sandwiches by matching the word provided with a word from the Spelling List that means the same or almost the same.

1. quarrel	2. hint
3. alike	4. student
5. perform	6. café
7. versus	8. foretell
9. joining	10. command

Name _____ Date _____

Word Stretchers

Part 1: Stretch the words by making them plural.

Word	Plural
pupil	
community	
university	
union	
refugee	
dictionary	
dictator	

Part 2: Stretch the words by adding -s, -ed, and -ing.

Word	Add -s	Add -ed	Add -ing
uniform			
argue			
cue			
commute			
execute			
dictate			
predict			

Word Stretchers

Part 3: The prefix *semi-* means half or partly. Stretch the words in the first column by adding the prefix *semi-* and writing the words in the second column. Then match the words with their meanings by writing the letter of the meaning in the third column.

Word	Word + Prefix *semi-*	Meaning
final	1.	
skilled	2.	
sweet	3.	
circle	4.	
pro	5.	
darkness	6.	

a. partly dark

b. more skilled than someone who has no skills, but less than someone who is skilled

c. a person who is paid for an activity, but relies only partly on this pay

d. the round or match that comes before the final one in a tournament

e. slightly sweet

f. half of a circle

Name _____   Date _____

Unit 14 Spelling List

Words that Follow the Rules

baboon	(ba-boon)
mushroom	(mush-room)
droop	(droop)
raccoon	(rac-coon)
youth	(youth)
group	(group)
fluent	(flu-ent)
inconclusive	(in-con-clu-sive)
exclude	(ex-clude)
rude	(rude)

Words with Prefixes: The prefix *mid-* means middle.

midday	(mid + day)	(mid-day)
midnight	(mid + night)	(mid-night)
midsummer	(mid + summer)	(mid-sum-mer)
midway	(mid + way)	(mid-way)

Related Words

tractor	(tract + or)	(trac-tor)
traction	(tract + ion)	(trac-tion)
subtract	(sub + tract)	(sub-tract)
distract	(dis + tract)	(dis-tract)

Spelling Dangers

luxury	(lux-u-ry)
deluxe	(de-luxe)

Proper Nouns

Illinois	(Il-li-nois)
Wyoming	(Wy-o-ming)

Name _____   Date _____

Get to Know the States
Illinois and Wyoming

Use the State Facts pages to complete Parts 1 and 2.

Part 1: Write the name of the state next to its capital.

CAPITAL	STATE
1. Cheyenne	_____
2. Springfield	_____

Part 2: Write a sentence for each state that includes one fact about the state. Be sure to include the name of the state in your sentence.

1. _____

   _____

2. _____

   _____

Bonus: Name the highest point in Wyoming and Illinois.

The highest point in _____ is _____ .

The highest point in _____ is _____ .

Name _____   Date _____

Antonym Antics and Prefix Practice

Part 1: Antonyms are words that are opposite in meaning. Find antonyms in the Spelling List for the words listed.

Word	Antonym
add	1.
rise up	2.
conclusive	3.
poverty	4.
polite	5.
include	6.
halting	7.

Part 2: The prefix *mid-* means middle. Write words with the prefix *mid-* that mean the same as the phrases below.

1. the middle of the night _____

2. the middle of the winter _____

3. the middle of the day _____

4. the middle of the year _____

5. halfway or in the middle of the distance _____

6. the middle of the summer _____

Name _____   Date _____

Word Sort

Part 1: Sort the Words that Follow the Rules and the words in the /oo/ Sound Word Bank according to their spelling of the /oo/ sound.

/oo/ Sound Word Bank				
troop	balloon	truth	soup	conclude
inclusive	intrude	exclusive	cartoon	include

oo	

ou	u	u-consonant-e

Part 2: Select two of the words and use each in a sentence.

Word   **Sentence**

_____   _____

                                        _____

_____   _____

                                        _____

Name _____   Date _____

Super Scavenger Hunt

Find the words in the Spelling List that fit the clues. Some words are used more than once.

1. two words that start and end with a vowel _____

   _____

2. a word that starts and ends with the same letter _____

3. two words that end in *y* _____ _____

4. six words that begin with a prefix _____

   _____ _____ _____

   _____ _____

5. a word in which *x* sounds like k as /k/ _____

6. the names of two wild animals _____

   _____

7. two rhyming words _____ _____

8. a word that rhymes with actor _____

9. a word that rhymes with truth _____

10. a word that means "the power to grip a surface when moving"

    _____

11. twelve o'clock at night _____

Name _____   Date _____

Unit 15 Spelling List

Words that Follow the Rules

concern	(con-cern)
observe	(ob-serve)
internal	(in-ter-nal)
early	(ear-ly)
learn	(learn)
disturb	(dis-turb)
absurd	(ab-surd)
survive	(sur-vive)
firm	(firm)
thirsty	(thirs-ty)

Words with Prefixes: The prefix *fore-* means before.

forecast	(fore + cast)	(fore-cast)
forewarn	(fore + warn)	(fore-warn)
foresee	(fore + see)	(fore-see)
forefather	(fore + father)	(fore-fath-er)

Related Words

ferry	(fer + ry)	(fer-ry)
conference	(con + fer + ence)	(con-fer-ence)
prefer	(pre + fer)	(pre-fer)
transfer	(trans + fer)	(trans-fer)

Spelling Dangers

business	(busi-ness)
figure	(fig-ure)

Proper Nouns

Vermont	(Ver-mont)
Alaska	(A-las-ka)

Name _____   Date _____

Get to Know the States
Vermont and Alaska

Use the State Facts pages to complete Parts 1 and 2.

Part 1: Write the name of the state next to its capital.

CAPITAL	STATE
1. Juneau	_____
2. Montpelier	_____

Part 2: Write a sentence for each state that includes one fact about the state. Be sure to include the name of the state in your sentence.

1. _____

   _____

2. _____

   _____

Bonus: Give the dates when Alaska and Vermont became part of the United States of America.

_____ became a state on _____ .

_____ became a state on _____ .

Name _____   Date _____

Supply the Missing Letters

Put a check in the column with the letters that correctly complete the word in the first column. Write the word in the last column.

Word	er	ir	ur	ear	Spelling Word
obs__ve					1.
f__m					2.
dist__b					3.
conc__n					4.
th__sty					5.
abs__d					6.
___ly					7.
s__vive					8.
l___n					9.
int__nal					10.

Name _____   Date _____

It Comes Before

Part 1: Use spelling words to answer the following.

1. Which word comes first in alphabetical order? _____

2. The words "Do not ___" come before which word to indicate that someone or something should not be bothered? _____

3. All the words on the list come before this word alphabetically. What is the word? _____

4. Which word has a prefix that means "before" and does NOT start with *fore-*? _____

5. Which word comes before "eight" when describing a shape you can make when skating? _____

6. Which word comes before "bird" in the saying, "The ___ bird gets the worm"? _____

7. Before a bridge has been built to connect an island to a mainland, what might you take to get back and forth between the two? _____

8. What might you have with your parents to get their opinions before you make an important decision? _____

9. The words "it's none of your ___ " come before which word to mean that you don't need to bother or worry? _____

10. Which word has a prefix that means "across" before a root that means to "carry or bring"? _____

It Comes Before

Part 2: The prefix *fore-* means before. Write the words with the prefix *fore-* that mean the same as the phrases.

1. ancestor or family member who lived before you _____

2. predict the weather or events that are to come _____

3. ability to look ahead (see) and plan for the future _____

4. warn someone of danger before it happens _____

Name _____   Date _____

The *r* Rules the Words

Part 1: Sort the Words that Follow the Rules and the words in the r-Controlled Word Bank by their spelling of the /er/ sound.

r-Controlled Word Bank				
birthday	misery	burden	superb	search
research	earth	dirty	hurry	birdbath

er	ur

ir	ear

Part 2: List the five other words in the Spelling List that contain the /er/ sound. Circle the letters in each word that make the sound.

_____   _____

_____   _____

Name _____   Date _____

Unit 16 Spelling List

Words that Follow the Rules

skeleton	(skel-e-ton)
package	(pack-age)
octopus	(oc-to-pus)
arctic	(arc-tic)
campus	(cam-pus)
ache	(ache)
mechanic	(me-chan-ic)
chorus	(chor-us)
character	(char-ac-ter)
stomach	(stom-ach)

Words with Prefixes: The prefix *under-* means beneath or below.

underpass	(under + pass)	(un-der-pass)
undersea	(under + sea)	(un-der-sea)
underground	(under + ground)	(un-der-ground)
undertake	(under + take)	(un-der-take)

Related Words

vision	(vis + ion)	(vi-sion)
visible	(vis + ible)	(vis-i-ble)
invisible	(in + vis + ible)	(in-vis-i-ble)
vista	(vis + ta)	(vis-ta)

Spelling Dangers

journal	(jour-nal)
courtesy	(cour-te-sy)

Proper Nouns

Montana	(Mon-tan-a)
Colorado	(Col-o-ra-do)

Name _____   Date _____

Get to Know the States
Montana and Colorado

Use the State Facts pages to complete Parts 1 and 2.

Part 1: Write the name of the state next to its capital.

CAPITAL	STATE
1. Denver	_____
2. Helena	_____

Part 2: Write a sentence for each state that includes one fact about the state. Be sure to include the name of the state in your sentence.

1. _____

_____

2. _____

_____

Bonus: Name the mountain range found in Colorado and Montana.

The _____ are found in _____ .

The _____ are found in _____ .

Name _____   Date _____

Backward, Below, and Beneath

Part 1: Unscramble the letters to spell Words that Follow the Rules; but be careful, the letters of a mystery word are woven in as well. Write the words on the lines and circle any extra letters that you find. When you finish, start at the end and read backward to find the mystery word.

dskeletonnmechanicucampusochorusrachegpackager stomacheoctopusdarcticncharacteru

1. _____

2. _____

3. _____

4. _____

5. _____

6. _____

7. _____

8. _____

9. _____

10. _____

The mystery word is _____ .

Backward, Below, and Beneath

Part 2: The prefix *under-* means beneath or below. Choose a word from the *Under-* Word Bank to match each phrase below.

Under- Word Bank		
undertake	undershirt	undersea
underground	underside	underpass

1. beneath the surface of the earth _____

2. a passageway that goes beneath a highway _____

3. to take upon oneself _____

4. beneath the surface of the sea _____

5. a collarless shirt worn next to the body _____

6. the side or surface that is underneath _____

Name _____   Date _____

The Four Spellings of /k/

Sort the Words that Follow the Rules and the words in the /k/ Sound Word Bank by their spelling of the /k/ sound. Hint: Two words have two spellings of /k/.

/k/ Sound Word Bank				
squeak	ankle	chuckle	consume	blackbird
toothpick	hockey	brake	include	cheek

k	ck

c	ch

Name _____ Date _____

Complete the Sentence

Use a spelling word to complete each sentence.

1. We go to the eye doctor to have our _____ checked.

2. Robinson Crusoe kept a _____ of his daily experiences on the deserted island.

3. This new tape is so clear that it appears to be _____ when used.

4. A younger person usually holds the door for an older person as a

   _____ .

5. The _____ region is the area around the north pole.

6. My cousin was barely _____ in her costume; only her eyes could be seen.

7. As we looked down the lane of trees to the hillside beyond, the

   _____ was beautiful.

8. Our neighborhood _____ often competes in singing contests.

9. After playing kickball for hours, my ankle began to _____ .

10. I can't wait to unwrap the _____ to find out what's inside.

11. Our _____ provides a framework for our muscles and organs.

Complete the Sentence

12. In the future we may be able to live underwater and may even build

an _____ city.

13. My _____ did flip-flops when we rode the roller coaster.

14. Wilbur is my favorite _____ in *Charlotte's Web*.

15. Subway trains travel _____ .

Name _____   Date _____

Unit 17 Spelling List

Words that Follow the Rules

squirrel	(squir-rel)
requested	(re-ques-ted)
conquest	(con-quest)
quietly	(qui-et-ly)
quarterly	(quar-ter-ly)
quotation	(quo-ta-tion)
special	(spe-cial)
official	(of-fi-cial)
social	(so-cial)
artificial	(ar-ti-fi-cial)

Words with Prefixes: The prefix *de-* means opposite or remove.

deface	(de + face)	(de-face)
declaw	(de + claw)	(de-claw)
dethrone	(de + throne)	(de-throne)
defrost	(de + frost)	(de-frost)

Related Words

current	(cur + rent)	(cur-rent)
cursive	(cur + sive)	(cur-sive)
currency	(cur + rency)	(cur-ren-cy)
concur	(con + cur)	(con-cur)

Spelling Dangers

honor	(hon-or)
donor	(do-nor)

Proper Nouns

Arizona	(Ar-i-zo-na)
Delaware	(Del-a-ware)

Name _____   Date _____

Get to Know the States
Arizona and Delaware

Use the State Facts pages to complete Parts 1 and 2.

Part 1: Write the name of the state next to its capital.

	CAPITAL		STATE
1.	Dover		_____
2.	Phoenix		_____

Part 2: Write a sentence for each state that includes one fact about the state. Be sure to include the name of the state in your sentence.

1. _____

   _____

2. _____

   _____

Bonus: Name the lowest point in Delaware and Arizona.

_____ is the lowest point in _____.

_____ is the lowest point in _____.

Name _____ Date _____

Patterns and Prefixes

Part 1: Sort the Words that Follow the Rules and the words in the Pattern Word Bank according to the pattern they match.

Pattern Word Bank				
facial	question	judicial	quality	require
tranquil	financial	acquire	superficial	quantity

/kw/ Sound Spelled *qu*	

/shul/ Sound Spelled *cial*	

Patterns and Prefixes

Part 2: The prefix *de-* means opposite or remove. Write the words with the prefix *de-* that match the phrases below.

1. remove frost by thawing _____

2. take away the looks of a building or statue _____

3. remove the claws from the feet _____

4. remove from the throne _____

Bonus: What does deodorant do? _____

_____

Name _____   Date _____

What Am I?

Match the words in the first column with their meanings in the second column.
Write the letter of the meaning on the lines provided.

_____   1. conquest   a. friendly

_____   2. honor   b. money in use

_____   3. current   c. person in authority

_____   4. social   d. passage that is quoted

_____   5. currency   e. a person who gives

_____   6. donor   f. different from others

_____   7. squirrel   g. gained by force

_____   8. official   h. flow of electricity

_____   9. quotation   i. respect

_____   10. special   j. small rodent with a long bushy tail

Name _____   Date _____

Spotting Errors in Spelling

Circle the misspelled word in each sentence and write the corrected word on the line.

1. In our town, we honer our police officers and fire fighters.

   _____

2. Will Mom concir with our plans for a vacation in Florida?

   _____

3. The curent news is reported in the daily paper.

   _____

4. Delawear is the second smallest state in the United States.

   _____

5. The squirel buried acorns in the garden.

   _____

6. Dad was a blood doner at the hospital yesterday.

   _____

7. Part of the Grand Canyon is found in Arazona.

   _____

Spotting Errors in Spelling

8. We studied the curency of other countries in history.

   _____

9. There was a speshul notice in the paper about the parade.

   _____

10. I wrote the essay in cersive for the English assignment.

    _____

11. We rekwested sprinkles on our ice cream.

    _____

12. The magazine is delivered quatterly.

    _____

13. The vandals used spray paint to defase the front of the building.

    _____

14. We played quitely so we didn't wake the baby.

    _____

15. "Home on the Range" is the offishul state song of Kansas.

    _____

Name _____ Date _____

Unit 18 Spelling List

Words that Review Spelling Rules

cubicle	(cu-bi-cle)
fumigate	(fu-mi-gate)
frugal	(fru-gal)
swoop	(swoop)
mockingbird	(mock-ing-bird)
curb	(curb)
choral	(chor-al)
quail	(quail)
squirm	(squirm)
crucial	(cru-cial)

Words that Review Prefixes

foretell	(fore + tell)	(fore-tell)
underline	(under + line)	(un-der-line)
deform	(de + form)	(de-form)
midstream	(mid + stream)	(mid-stream)

Words that Review Related Words

cursor	(cur + sor)	(cur-sor)
visual	(vis + ual)	(vis-u-al)
transferable	(trans + fer + able)	(trans-fer-a-ble)
dictating	(dic + tating)	(dic-ta-ting)

Name _____   Date _____

Get to Know the States Review

Write the name of the state next to its capital.

CAPITAL   STATE

1. Cheyenne   _____

2. Denver   _____

3. Juneau   _____

4. Dover   _____

5. Phoenix   _____

6. Helena   _____

7. Atlanta   _____

8. Springfield   _____

9. Montpelier   _____

10. Richmond   _____

Bonus: Write the two-letter postal abbreviation after each state name. For example: New York NY

Name _____   Date _____

Synonym Sort and Prefix Practice

Part 1: Sort the words in the word box into pairs of synonyms.
Hint: Synonyms are words that mean the same or almost the same.

squirm	important	frugal	dive	fidget
ledge	swoop	curb	crucial	thrifty

_____ and _____

_____ and _____

_____ and _____

_____ and _____

_____ and _____

Part 2: Find the word in the Word Bank that answers the question. Write the word or words on the line and circle the prefix.

Word Bank		
foretell	midstream	undersea
underline	semisoft	deform

1. Which two words have a prefix that means "below" or "beneath"?

   _____   _____

2. Which word has a prefix that means "middle"?

   _____

Synonym Sort and Prefix Practice

3. Which word has a prefix that means "opposite" or "remove"?

   _____

4. Which word has a prefix that means "half" or "partly"?

   _____

5. Which word has a prefix that means "before"? _____

Name _____ Date _____

Spelling Dangers

Find the words in the Spelling Dangers Word Bank that fit the clues. Write the words on the line or lines after the clues.

Spelling Dangers Word Bank				
against	luxury	business	donor	journal
deluxe	courtesy	honor	restaurant	figure

1. the *au* sounds like the *a* in *ago* _____

2. *ai* sounds like short *e* _____

3. *x* sounds like /k/ and the *u* has a *zha* sound _____

4. the *our* has the sound of /er/ _____

5. the *o* is long and the *or* sounds like /er/ _____

6. *bus* sounds like *biz* _____

7. *x* sounds like /k/ and the *u* is short even though there is a silent *e*

   _____

8. the *our* has the sound of /er/ and *y* sounds like long *e*

   _____

9. the *ure* sounds like /yer/ _____

10. the *h* is silent and the *or* sounds like /er/ _____

Name _____   Date _____

Crossword Fun

Use words from the Spelling List to solve the puzzle.

Crossword Fun

Across

4. migratory bird
6. separation between sidewalk and street; ledge
8. important
9. able to be carried from one place to another
12. twist like a worm
14. to spoil the surface of
15. speaking to a person or reading to them
16. thrifty

Down

1. a small work space
2. something that can be seen
3. in the middle of a stream.
5. draw a line below
7. a bird that imitates or mocks other birds
8. movable marker on a computer screen
10. apply smoke to rid of germs or insects
11. relating to a chorus
12. move with a sweep; dive
13. to predict

Unit 19 Spelling List

Words that Follow the Rules
trivia   (triv-i-a)
piano   (pi-an-o)
memorial   (me-mo-ri-al)
librarian   (li-brar-i-an)
champion   (cham-pi-on)
curiosity   (cu-ri-os-i-ty)
patriot   (pa-tri-ot)
radio   (ra-di-o)
machine   (ma-chine)
period   (pe-ri-od)

Words with Suffixes: The suffix *-able* means capable of, worthy of, or inclined to.
respectable   (respect + able)   (re-spec-ta-ble)
predictable   (predict + able)   (pre-dict-a-ble)
acceptable   (accept + able)   (ac-cep-ta-ble)
honorable   (honor + able)   (hon-or-a-ble)

Related Words
adventure   (ad + ven + ture)   (ad-ven-ture)
venture   (ven + ture)   (ven-ture)
avenue   (a + ven + ue)   (av-en-ue)
convention   (con + ven + tion)   (con-ven-tion)

Spelling Dangers
February   (Feb-ru-ar-y)
animals   (an-i-mals)

Proper Nouns
Louisiana   (Lou-i-si-an-a)
Hawaii   (Ha-wai-i)

Name _____   Date _____

Get to Know the States
Louisiana and Hawaii

Use the State Facts pages to complete Parts 1 and 2.

Part 1: Write the name of the state next to its capital.

	CAPITAL	STATE
1.	Honolulu	_____
2.	Baton Rouge	_____

Part 2: Write a sentence for each state that includes one fact about the state. Be sure to include the name of the state in your sentence.

1. _____

   _____

2. _____

   _____

Bonus: Name the state tree for Hawaii and Louisiana.

The _____ is the state tree of _____ .

The _____ is the state tree of _____ .

<u>Name</u> _____ <u>Date</u> _____

Complete the Sentence

Use a spelling word to complete each sentence.

1. Use a _____ at the end of a declarative sentence.

2. The _____ will help us find a book to use for our report.

3. To prepare for her recital, my sister practices the _____ twice a day.

4. For many explorers, a sense of _____ has led to great discoveries.

5. The rain was _____ given the clouds, thunder, and lightning.

6. My friends and I like to listen to our favorite songs on the

   _____ .

7. My brother won first prize in the chess tournament and is now state

   _____ .

8. Mark won the quiz show because he knows a lot of _____ .

9. When visiting a museum or art gallery, it is important to behave in a

   _____ manner.

10. My mother sews all of our clothes on her sewing _____ .

11. Our town plans to build a _____ in honor of our first mayor.

Complete the Sentence

12. I like to read _____ stories that tell of danger and brave deeds.

13. Comic book collectors are coming to our town for a _____ where they can talk about the stories and characters in their magazines.

14. A _____ shows his love of country by his actions.

15. A nature park can be home to many different kinds of

    _____.

16. The parade will travel down the _____ from the town square to the town hall.

17. Setting out to sea alone on the raft was a risky _____.

18. Judge Greene was elected because he is the most _____ man in town.

19. Chocolate cake is my favorite, but when I'm hungry, any flavor cake is

    _____.

20. Presidents' Day, as well as the birthdays of Washington and Lincoln, is

    celebrated in _____ .

Name _____   Date _____

Synonym Sandwiches and the Suffix *-able*

Part 1: Put the tops on the synonym sandwiches by matching the word provided with a word from the Spelling List that means the same or almost the same.

1.	2.
monument	fighter

3.	4.
nosiness	noble

5.	6.
creatures	satisfactory

7.	8.
boulevard	adventure

9.	10.
decent	meeting

Synonym Sandwiches and the Suffix *-able*

Part 2: The suffix *-able* means capable of, worthy of, or inclined to. Write the word with the suffix *-able* that means the same as the phrases below.

1. worthy of esteem or respect _____

2. worth accepting _____

3. worthy of honor _____

4. capable of being foretold or predicted _____

5. capable of providing comfort _____

Name _____   Date _____

Unit 20 Spelling List

Words that Follow the Rules

science   (sci-ence)
scene   (scene)
conceited   (con-ceit-ed
ancestor   (an-ces-tor)
absence   (ab-sence)
citizen   (cit-i-zen)
rejoice   (re-joice)
twice   (twice)
fragrance   (fra-grance)
recent   (re-cent)

Words with Suffixes: The suffix -ly means in what manner (how).

harshly   (harsh + ly)   (harsh-ly)
loudly   (loud + ly)   (loud-ly)
decently   (decent + ly)   (de-cent-ly)
silently   (silent + ly)   (si-lent-ly)

Related Words

script   (script)   (script)
description   (de + script + ion)   (de-scrip-tion)
prescription   (pre + script + ion) (pre-scrip-tion)
manuscript   (manu + script)   (man-u-script)

Spelling Dangers

toward   (to-ward)
permanent   (per-ma-nent)

Proper Nouns

Indiana   (In-di-an-a)
Missouri   (Mis-sou-ri)

Name _____   Date _____

Get to Know the States
Indiana and Missouri

Use the State Facts pages to complete Parts 1 and 2.

Part 1: Write the name of the state next to its capital.

CAPITAL   STATE

1. Jefferson City   _____

2. Indianapolis   _____

Part 2: Write a sentence for each state that includes one fact about the state. Be sure to include the name of the state in your sentence.

1. _____

_____

2. _____

_____

Bonus: Find the nicknames for Missouri and Indiana.

_____ is the nickname for _____ .

_____ is the nickname for _____ .

Name _____ Date _____

Dictionary Skills

Part 1: Write the spelling words that would be found on the dictionary pages with the following pairs of guide words.

scheme	scooter
1.	

amuse	and
2.	

tutor	twist
3.	

fowl	fraud
4.	

concave	concert
5.	

derail	desperate
6.	

perfect	permission
7.	

minus	mist
8.	

Part 2: Put the following words in alphabetical order.

scene   1. _____

recent   2. _____

citizen   3. _____

rejoice   4. _____

manuscript   5. _____

toward   6. _____

absence   7. _____

silently   8. _____

script   9. _____

Indiana   10.

Dictionary Skills

Part 3: Write the spelling word that matches each definition. You may use a dictionary.

1. a person who lives in a city _____

2. the place where an event occurs _____

3. without noise _____

4. two times _____

5. a written direction for the preparation and use of a medicine

    _____

6. in a rough manner _____

7. lasting _____

8. handwriting _____

9. vain or proud _____

10. to be happy _____

Name _____   Date _____

/s/ Sort and Suffix *-ly*

Part 1: Sort the words in the Spelling List according to their spelling of /s/. Some words contain two spellings.

Hint: Don't get tricked by *scr*. *Scr-* is a blend.

/s/ Spelled *sc*	/s/ Spelled *c* Followed by *i*

/s/ Spelled *c* Followed by *e*	

Part 2: The suffix *-ly* means in what manner. Add the suffix *-ly* to the words below, then use the new words you made in the sentences that follow.

1. loud _____

2. silent _____

3. decent _____

4. kind _____

/s/ Sort and Suffix -ly

5. harsh _____

6. soft _____

7. The old man spoke _____ to the dog and the dog wagged its tail and licked the man's hand.

8. The girl stroked the kitten's fur _____ while the kitten purred.

9. The bell rang _____ and woke the sleeping firefighters.

10. The wind whipped _____ and blew the sand into hills and valleys.

11. Not a sound could be heard as the snow fell _____ .

12. The men were paid _____ for their long hours of work.

Name _____   Date _____

Unit 21 Spelling List

Words that Follow the Rules

balanced	(bal-anced)
relieved	(re-lieved)
motivated	(mo-ti-vat-ed)
sharing	(shar-ing)
probing	(prob-ing)
likely	(like-ly)
immediately	(im-me-di-ate-ly)
tasteful	(taste-ful)
announcement	(an-nounce-ment)
sincerely	(sin-cere-ly)

Words with Suffixes: The suffix *-ation* means state or condition of being.

starvation	(starv + ation)	(star-va-tion)
occupation	(occup + ation)	(oc-cu-pa-tion)
humiliation	(humili + ation)	(hu-mil-i-a-tion)
location	(loc + ation)	(lo-ca-tion)

Related Words

capture	(cap + ture)	(cap-ture)
captivate	(cap + tivate)	(cap-ti-vate)
captor	(cap + tor)	(cap-tor)
captive	(cap + tive)	(cap-tive)

Spelling Dangers

language	(lan-guage)
caught	(caught)

Proper Nouns

West Virginia	(West Vir-gin-ia)
North Carolina	(North Car-o-li-na)

Name _____   Date _____

Get to Know the States
West Virginia and North Carolina

Use the State Facts pages to complete Parts 1 and 2.

Part 1: Write the name of the state next to its capital.

CAPITAL	STATE
1. Raleigh	_____
2. Charleston	_____

Part 2: Write a sentence for each state that includes one fact about the state. Be sure to include the name of the state in your sentence.

1. _____

_____

2. _____

_____

Bonus: Name one agricultural product found in North Carolina and one found in West Virginia.

_____ is found in _____ .

_____ is found in _____ .

Name _____   Date _____

Synonyms and Sentences

Part 1: Find the spelling word that means the same or almost the same as the word or words below. You may use a dictionary or thesaurus. Write the spelling word on the line.

1. exploring   _____

2. prisoner   _____

3. job   _____

4. at once   _____

5. relaxed or comforted   _____

6. declaration   _____

7. take or seize   _____

8. truthfully   _____

9. pleasing   _____

10. probable or possible   _____

Synonyms and Sentences

Part 2: Find a spelling word to complete each sentence. Write the spelling word on the line.

1. When my brother and I went fishing, he _____ a large striped bass.

2. The juggler _____ a spinning bowl on his head while spinning rings on both arms and one leg.

3. The little lost dog seemed to _____ everyone and several people offered to take it home.

4. The coach _____ the players by reminding them that the championship game would be played soon.

5. I speak English, so when I learn Spanish it will be the second

   _____ I know.

6. I always pack extra food when we go on a picnic because I enjoy

   _____ with others.

7. The prisoner tried to escape from his _____ by hiding in the forest.

8. Without any food to eat, the animals were in danger of

   _____ .

9. We followed the treasure map to find the _____ of the gold.

10. It was difficult for the boy to forget the _____ he felt when the other boys made fun of him.

Name _____   Date _____

Suffix Scramble

Part 1: Add the suffix in the second column to the base word in the first. Put a check in the column that tells what you must do to the base word when you add that suffix. Write the word with the suffix in the final column. The first one has been done for you.

Base Word	Add the Suffix	Drop the e	Keep the e	Words that Follow the Rules
1. taste	-ful		√	tasteful
2. relieve	-ed			
3. sincere	-ly			
4. share	-ing			
5. announce	-ment			
6. immediate	-ly			
7. motivate	-ed			
8. probe	-ing			
9. like	-ly			
10. balance	-ed			

Part 2: Use the rules that you have learned to add suffixes to these Related Words.

1. capture	-ing		
2. captivate	-ed		
3. capture	-ed		
4. captivate	-ing		

Suffix Scramble

Part 3: The suffix -ation means the state or condition of being. Choose the word with that suffix that matches each meaning.

humiliation	starvation	desperation
occupation	inspiration	location

1. the state of being located _____

2. the condition of not having enough to eat _____

3. the condition of having one's pride taken away _____

4. the state of being inspired or encouraged _____

5. the state of being occupied (having a job) _____

6. the state of feeling hopeless or desperate _____

Name   Date

Unit 22 Spelling List

Words that Follow the Rules
heavier   (heav-i-er)
laziest   (la-zi-est)
cozier   (co-zi-er)
tiniest   (ti-ni-est)
worrying   (wor-ry-ing)
supplying   (sup-ply-ing)
displaying   (dis-play-ing)
betrayed   (be-trayed)
surveyed   (sur-veyed)
relaying   (re-lay-ing)

Words with Suffixes: The suffix *-ist* means one who practices.
dentist   (dent + ist)   (den-tist)
journalist   (journal + ist)   (jour-nal-ist)
scientist   (scient + ist)   (sci-en-tist)
violinist   (violin + ist)   (vi-o-lin-ist)

Related Words
credible   (cred + ible)   (cred-i-ble)
incredible   (in + cred + ible)   (in-cred-i-ble)
credit   (cred + it)   (cred-it)
discredit   (dis + cred + it)   (dis-cred-it)

Spelling Dangers
prairie   (prai-rie)
daily   (dai-ly)

Proper Nouns
California   (Cal-i-for-nia)
Minnesota   (Min-ne-so-ta)

Name _____   Date _____

Get to Know the States
Minnesota and California

Use the State Facts pages to complete Parts 1 and 2.

Part 1: Write the name of the state next to its capital.

CAPITAL	STATE
1. St. Paul	_____
2. Sacramento	_____

Part 2: Write a sentence for each state that includes one fact about the state. Be sure to include the name of the state in your sentence.

1. _____

   _____

2. _____

   _____

Bonus: Name the body of water that borders California and the body of water that borders Minnesota.

_____ borders _____.

_____ borders _____.

Name _____ Date _____

Suffix Scramble

Part 1: Add the suffix in the second column to the base word in the first. Put a check in the column that tells what you must do to the base word when you add that suffix. Write the word with the suffix in the final column. The first one has been done for you.

Base Word	Add the Suffix	Change the *y* to *i*	Keep the *y*	Words that Follow the Rules
1. relay	*-ing*		√	relaying
2. heavy	*-er*			
3. betray	*-ed*			
4. worry	*-ing*			
5. tiny	*-est*			
6. lazy	*-est*			
7. survey	*-ed*			
8. display	*-ing*			
9. cozy	*-er*			
10. supply	*-ing*			

Part 2: Use the rules that you have learned to add suffixes to these words.

1. chunky	*-est*			
2. portray	*-ed*			
3. silly	*-er*			
4. imply	*-ing*			

Suffix Scramble

Part 3: The suffix *-ist* means one who practices: performs, does, makes. Choose the word with that suffix that matches each meaning.

chemist	dentist	cyclist	tourist
journalist	machinist	violinist	scientist

1. a person trained in chemistry _____

2. a person whose profession is the care and treatment of teeth

   _____

3. a person who is an expert in science _____

4. a person who rides a cycle or a bicycle _____

5. a person who travels for pleasure _____

6. a person who reports the news _____

7. a person who plays the violin _____

8. a person who makes or works on machines _____

Name _____ Date _____

I Know What You Mean

Find the spelling words that mean the same as the underlined word or words in the sentences.

1. The craft store will be <u>providing</u> the materials for the Boy Scout project.

    _____

2. Cuddled together, it was hard to tell which puppy was <u>more comfortable</u>.

    _____

3. The evil prince tried to <u>spoil the good reputation of</u> his father, the king.

    _____

4. The <u>person who plays a violin</u> will give a concert today.

    _____

5. All during the storm I was <u>feeling concerned</u> about you.

    _____

6. Antelope and buffalo roam the <u>grassland</u>.

    _____

7. The <u>person who knows about science</u> will perform the experiment.

    _____

8. Which of the two stacks of books looks <u>more hefty</u>?

I Know What You Mean

9. The <u>person who reports the news</u> will interview the author.

   _____

10. Snow in July would be <u>unbelievable</u>.

    _____

11. My best friend and I talk <u>every day</u>.

    _____

12. The toy store is <u>showing off</u> roller blades in their window this week.

    _____

13. We <u>examined</u> the damage caused by the forest fire.

    _____

14. I have an appointment with the <u>person who cares for people's teeth</u> on Friday.

    _____

15. Which of the five hamsters is the <u>smallest</u>?

    _____

16. Three teams will be <u>sending along in stages</u> the message by phone.

    _____

17. I know the boy's story about the white tiger is <u>reliable</u> because I saw it also.

I Know What You Mean

18. We read a funny story about three dogs who each tried to prove that he was the <u>most unwilling to work</u>.

   _____

19. The pirate <u>double-crossed</u> his shipmates by telling where they hid the gold.

   _____

20. George deserves <u>praise</u> for saving the baby by catching the runaway stroller.

   _____

Name _____   Date _____

Unit 23 Spelling List

Words that Follow the Rules

journeys	(jour-neys)
highways	(high-ways)
holidays	(hol-i-days)
turkeys	(tur-keys)
valleys	(val-leys)
diaries	(di-a-ries)
hobbies	(hob-bies)
libraries	(li-brar-ies)
counties	(coun-ties)
territories	(ter-ri-to-ries)

Words with Suffixes: The suffix *-or* means one who.

senator	(senate – e + or)	(sen-a-tor)
governor	(govern + or)	(gov-er-nor)
director	(direct + or)	(di-rec-tor)
counselor	(counsel + or)	(coun-se-lor)

Related Words

sense	(sens + e)	(sense)
sensitive	(sens + itive)	(sen-si-tive)
sensational	(sens + ational)	(sen-sa-tion-al)
nonsense	(non + sens + e)	(non-sense)

Spelling Dangers

really	(real-ly)
everybody	(eve-ry-bod-y)

Proper Nouns

Massachusetts	(Mas-sa-chu-setts)
Washington	(Wash-ing-ton)

Name _____   Date _____

Get to Know the States
Massachusetts and Washington

Use the State Facts pages to complete Parts 1 and 2.

Part 1: Write the name of the state next to its capital.

	CAPITAL	STATE
1.	Olympia	_____
2.	Boston	_____

Part 2: Write a sentence for each state that includes one fact about the state. Be sure to include the name of the state in your sentence.

1. _____

   _____

2. _____

   _____

Bonus: Name the National Football League teams whose home arenas are in Massachusetts and Washington state.

The _____ play in _____ .

The _____ play in _____ .

<u>Name</u> _____ <u>Date</u> _____

Synonyms and Meanings

Find a spelling word that is a synonym for a word below or matches the meaning.

1. feel _____

2. gobblers _____

3. a member of a senate _____

4. trips _____

5. book collections _____

6. foolishness _____

7. everyone _____

8. roadways _____

9. lowlands found between ranges of mountains

   _____

10. journals _____

11. marvelous _____

12. lands under the rule of a government _____

13. manager _____

14. days of celebration _____

15. fun activities to do in one's free time _____

Synonyms and Meanings

16. quick to feel _____

17. state's chief executive _____

18. one who gives advice _____

19. very _____

20. divisions of states _____

Name _____   Date _____

Plurals and People

Part 1: Read the word in the first column. Decide what you have to do to the word to make it plural and put a check in that column. Write the plural in the final column. The first one has been done for you.

Base Word	To Make the Word Plural		Words that Follows the Rules
	Add -s	Change y to i and Add -es	
1. valley	√		valleys
2. territory			
3. journey			
4. diary			
5. county			
6. holiday			
7. library			
8. turkey			
9. hobby			
10. highway			

Plurals and People

Part 2: Follow the rules to make the following words plural.

Base Word	To Make the Word Plural		Plural Word
	Add -s	Change y to i and Add -es	
1. country			
2. tray			
3. candy			
4. birthday			
5. family			
6. dragonfly			
7. decoy			
8. cowboy			

Part 3: The suffix -or means one who. Match the words with the suffix -or with their meanings.

senator	director	governor
actor	counselor	donor

1. one who directs _____

2. one who governs _____

3. one who gives (donates) _____

4. one who acts _____

5. one who gives advice _____

6. one who is a member of the senate _____

Name _____   Date _____

Unit 24 Spelling List

Words that Review Spelling Rules

aviator	(a-vi-a-tor)
trio	(tri-o)
certain	(cer-tain)
turbulence	(tur-bu-lence)
expensive	(ex-pen-sive)
accurately	(ac-cu-rate-ly)
contributing	(con-trib-ut-ing)
countries	(coun-tries)
daisies	(dai-sies)
surveys	(sur-veys)

Words that Review Suffixes

relation	(rel + ation)	(re-la-tion)
slowly	(slow + ly)	(slow-ly)
educator	(educat + or)	(ed-u-ca-tor)
typist	(typ + ist)	(typ-ist)

Words that Review Related Words

sensitively	(sens + itively)	(sen-si-tive-ly)
credited	(cred + ited)	(cred-it-ed)
captured	(cap + tured)	(cap- tured)
prescriptions	(pre + scrip + tions)	(pre-scrip-tions)

Name _____   Date _____

Get to Know the States Review

Write the name of the state next to its capital.

CAPITAL   STATE

1. Jefferson City   _____

2. Charleston   _____

3. Sacramento   _____

4. Olympia   _____

5. Honolulu   _____

6. Indianapolis   _____

7. Boston   _____

8. Raleigh   _____

9. Baton Rouge   _____

10. St. Paul   _____

Bonus: Write the two-letter postal abbreviation after each state name. For example: New York NY

Name _____ Date _____

Spelling Rules and Suffixes

Part 1: Answer the questions with words from the Spelling List.

1. Which words formed their plural by changing *y* to *i* and adding *-es*?

   _____

2. Which words have a *c* that sounds like /s/?

   _____

3. Which word formed its plural by adding *-s*? _____

4. Which words dropped their silent *e* before adding a vowel suffix?

   _____

5. In which words does *i* have the sound of long *e*?

   _____

Spelling Rules and Suffixes

Part 2: Find the word in the Word Bank that answers the question. Write the word or words on the line and circle the suffix. You will use one word twice.

Word Bank		
typist	educator	slowly
honorable	relation	occupation

1. Which word has a suffix that changes an adjective to an adverb?

   _____

2. Which words have a suffix that means "a state of being"?

   _____

3. Which words have a suffix that tells the word names a person - "one who"?

   _____

4. Which word has a suffix that means "capable or worthy of"?

   _____

5. Which word has a suffix that means "in what manner (how)"?

   _____

Name _____ Date _____

Spelling Dangers

Find the words in the Spelling Dangers Word Bank that fit the clues.

Spelling Dangers Word Bank				
toward	really	animals	caught	permanent
February	daily	language	everybody	prairie

1. has a syllable that sounds like *gwij* _____

2. has a silent *r* and the *ar* sounds like *air* _____

3. has a silent *e* and two *y*'s that each sound like long *e*

   _____

4. has a *w* that is often not pronounced and then this word sounds like *tord*

   _____

5. has a *y* that sounds like long *e* and *ai* that sounds like long *a*

   _____

6. has *air* in it and a silent *i* _____

7. has an *er* that sounds like /ur/ _____

8. has an *ea* and y that sound like long *e* _____

9. has an *a* that sounds like /u/ _____

10. has the /aw/ sound spelled *au* _____

Name _____   Date _____

Crossword Fun

Use words from the Spelling List to solve the puzzle.

Crossword Fun

Across
1. nations
3. a group of three
6. correctly
9. state of being related or connected
12. written instructions of a doctor regarding type and dosage of medicine for a patient
16. giving or supplying
17. (acting or speaking) with feeling or concern

Down
2. in a slow way
4. costly
5. disturbance or state of unrest
7. flier
8. given credit; be considered favorably
10. caught
11. flowers that have white petals around a yellow center
13. sure; known to be true
14. one who types or uses a keyboard
15. looks over

Which spelling word is a synonym for teacher? _____

Name _____ Date _____

Unit 25 Spelling List

Words that Follow the Rules

photograph	(pho-to-graph)
dolphin	(dol-phin)
hyphen	(hy-phen)
philosophy	(phi-los-o-phy)
trophy	(tro-phy)
guilty	(guil-ty)
guard	(guard)
guitar	(gui-tar)
guess	(guess)
guide	(guide)

Words with Suffixes: The suffix *-ness* means condition or state.

forgiveness	(forgive + ness)	(for-give-ness)
closeness	(close + ness)	(close-ness)
goodness	(good + ness)	(good-ness)
illness	(ill + ness)	(ill-ness)

Related Words

audio	(aud + io)	(au-di-o)
audible	(aud + ible)	(au-di-ble)
audience	(aud + ience)	(au-di-ence)
audition	(aud + ition)	(au-di-tion)

Spelling Dangers

opposite	(op-po-site)
favorite	(fa-vor-ite)

Proper Nouns

South Dakota	(South Da-ko-ta)
Idaho	(I-da-ho)

Name _____   Date _____

Get to Know the States
South Dakota and Idaho

Use the State Facts pages to complete Parts 1 and 2.

Part 1: Write the name of the state next to its capital.

CAPITAL	STATE
1. Boise	_____
2. Pierre	_____

Part 2: Write a sentence for each state that includes one fact about the state. Be sure to include the name of the state in your sentence.

1. _____

_____

2. _____

_____

Bonus: Name the state or states that border Idaho and South Dakota to the south.

_____ is south of _____ .

_____

are south of _____ .

_____

Name _____   Date _____

Synonyms, Suffixes, and Scrambled Words

Part 1: Find a spelling word that means the same or almost the same as the word or words below. You may use a dictionary or thesaurus.

1. snapshot _____

2. protect _____

3. sickness _____

4. direct _____

5. prize _____

Part 2: The suffix *-ness* means condition or state. Choose the word with that suffix that matches each meaning.

goodness	friendliness	illness
sadness	forgiveness	closeness

1. condition of being friendly _____

2. state of being good, helpful, kind _____

3. condition of being near _____

4. state of being forgiven _____

5. condition of being sad or unhappy _____

6. condition of being sick _____

Synonyms, Suffixes, and Scrambled Words

Part 3: Unscramble the letters to make a spelling word that matches the clue given.

Scrambled Letters	Clue	Spelling Word
1. dabluie	able to be heard	
2. ofeairvt	best-liked	
3. suegs	to judge without all the facts	
4. tiylug	having done wrong	
5. pehhny	punctuation mark used to divide words	
6. syopholiph	study of ideas, right and wrong	
7. doaiu	relating to sound	
8. ruadg	one who defends	
9. tanidiou	opportunity for an actor to test his talents	
10. ratuig	musical instrument with six strings played by strumming	

Name _____ Date _____

Spotting Errors in Spelling

Circle the misspelled word in each sentence and write the corrected word on the line.

1. Our conversation was barely audibel over the loud music.

   _____

2. I have a dance audishun next Thursday. _____

3. The old fotograph was beginning to fade. _____

4. I will bring my guitare to the party and entertain the guests.

   _____

5. At camp, my teammates and I won the swimming trophee.

   _____

6. My favrite book is *Stone Fox*. _____

7. The people in the audients stood up and cheered at the end of the performance.

   _____

8. Please guyde us to the information desk because we are lost.

   _____

9. My friend's house is on the oposite side of the street from mine.

   _____

10. We asked my aunt's foorgivenes for breaking her lamp.

Spotting Errors in Spelling

11. The number twenty-one has a hiphin when written.

   _____

12. The audeo on my radio is broken so we can't listen to music.

   _____

13. My sister got to pet a dolfin at the aquarium. _____

14. He won't be able to attend the game due to ilness.

   _____

15. The woman was found giltee of shoplifting. _____

16. A man at the carnival said he could gess my weight.

   _____

17. It was amazing to see the clozeness of the canyon walls.

   _____

18. It is important to wear a seatbelt to gard against injury.

   _____

19. The old woman treated the children with gudness and care.

   _____

20. I hope to study filosophee in college.

Name   Date

Unit 26 Spelling List

Words that Follow the Rules

ointment	(oint-ment)
coil	(coil)
coinage	(coin-age)
poison	(poi-son)
exploit	(ex-ploit)
disappoint	(dis-ap-point)
employ	(em-ploy)
annoy	(an-noy)
royal	(roy-al)
voyage	(voy-age)

Words with Suffixes: The suffix *-ous* means full of, having.

hazardous	(hazard + ous)	(haz-ard-ous)
glamorous	(glamor + ous)	(glam-or-ous)
joyous	(joy + ous)	(joy-ous)
dangerous	(danger + ous)	(dan-ger-ous)

Related Words

form	(form)	(form)
formal	(form + al)	(for-mal)
formula	(form + ula)	(for-mu-la)
conform	(con + form)	(con-form)

Spelling Dangers

expect	(ex-pect)
beauty	(beau-ty)

Proper Nouns

Maryland	(Mary-land)
Oregon	(Or-e-gon)

Name _____   Date _____

Get to Know the States
Maryland and Oregon

Use the State Facts pages to complete Parts 1 and 2.

Part 1: Write the name of the state next to its capital.

CAPITAL   STATE

1. Salem   _____

2. Annapolis   _____

Part 2: Write a sentence for each state that includes one fact about the state. Be sure to include the name of the state in your sentence.

1. _____

   _____

2. _____

   _____

Bonus: Name the official state songs of Maryland and Oregon.

" _____ "

is the official state song of _____ .

" _____ "

is the official state song of _____ .

Name _____   Date _____

Word Sort

Part 1: Sort the Words that Follow the Rules and the words in the *oi* and *oy* Word Bank according to their spelling of the /oi/ sound.

oi and *oy* Word Bank				
destroy	rejoice	loin	avoid	decoy
hoist	gargoyle	loyal	convoy	broil

/oi/ Spelled *oi*		

/oi/ Spelled *oy*		

Part 2: Select two of the words and use each in a sentence.

Word   **Sentence**

_____   _____

                       _____

_____   _____

                       _____

Name _____ Date _____

Suffixes and Word Stretchers

Part 1: The suffix *-ous* means full of, having. Add the suffix to the words below and write the meaning of the word on the line that follows. The first one has been done for you.

Hint: Don't forget that *glamour* drops the *u* when it adds *-ous*.

Word	Word + Suffix -ous	Meaning
1. hazard	hazardous	having dangers and risks
2. joy		
3. glamour		
4. danger		
5. mountain		
6. thunder		

Part 2: Stretch the word *form* by adding more letters to make new words. Read each clue and add the number of letters indicated to stretch *form* into a different spelling word.

Word + Letters	Clue	Spelling Word
1. form + two letters	carry out in an exact way	
2. form + three letters	a recipe	
3. form + three letters	to obey, or do as others do	

Bonus: Add five letters to *form* to make a word that means "the state of being in a shape or arrangement or form." Hint: Think of *occupation* and *relation*.

Name _____   Date _____

How Good Is Your Memory?

Try to remember the spelling word that fits the clue. If you can remember the word, write it on the first line after the clue. If you have to look at the Spelling List, write the word on the second line. When you have finished, count the answers you remembered and spelled correctly, then count the answers you spelled correctly after you looked at the Spelling List. Record your score at the end.

	I remembered the word	I looked for the word
1. This word describes kings and queens.	_____	_____
2. This is another word for *hire*.	_____	_____
3. This word means to bother.	_____	_____
4. This is another word for *a cream*.	_____	_____
5. This will make you very ill and could cause death.	_____	_____
6. You could take one of these on board a ship or a spacecraft.	_____	_____
7. If you twist a length of rope, this is what it will do.	_____	_____
8. This means to look for something likely to occur.	_____	_____
9. This is another word for *money made of metal*.	_____	_____

How Good Is Your Memory?

	I remembered the word	I looked for the word
10. If you fail to do the expected, you do this.	_____	_____
11. This is another word for *good looks*.	_____	_____
12. This is a daring act.	_____	_____
13. This word means to shape.	_____	_____
14. If you are happy, you are this.	_____	_____
15. This is a recipe or fixed way of doing something.	_____	_____

Number of correct answers I remembered: _____

Number of correct answers I looked up: _____

Name _____   Date _____

Unit 27 Spelling List

Words that Follow the Rules

bound	(bound)
surround	(sur-round)
scoundrel	(scoun-drel)
ounce	(ounce)
blouse	(blouse)
drowsy	(drow-sy)
drown	(drown)
rowdy	(row-dy)
clownish	(clown-ish)
allow	(al-low)

Words with Suffixes: The suffix *-ous* means full of, having.

victorious	(victory – y + i + ous)	(vic-tor-i-ous)
glorious	(glory – y + i + ous)	(glor-i-ous)
furious	(fury – y + i + ous)	(fur-i-ous)
various	(vary – y + i + ous)	(var-i-ous)

Related Words

pending	(pend + ing)	(pend-ing)
pendant	(pend + ant)	(pen-dant)
pendulum	(pend + ulum)	(pen-du-lum)
appendage	(ap + pend + age)	(ap-pen-dage)

Spelling Dangers

during	(dur-ing)
occur	(oc-cur)

Proper Nouns

Florida	(Flor-i-da)
Nebraska	(Ne-bras-ka)

Name _____   Date _____

Get to Know the States
Florida and Nebraska

Use the State Facts pages to complete Parts 1 and 2.

Part 1: Write the name of the state next to its capital.

	CAPITAL	STATE
1.	Lincoln	_____
2.	Tallahassee	_____

Part 2: Write a sentence for each state that includes one fact about the state. Be sure to include the name of the state in your sentence.

1. _____

_____

2. _____

_____

Bonus: Name the state or states that border Nebraska and Florida to the north.

_____ and _____ are north of

_____ .

_____ is north of _____ .

Name _____ Date _____

Word Sort

Part 1: Sort the Words That Follow the Rules and the words in the *ou* and *ow* Word Bank according to their spelling of the /ou/ sound.

ou and *ow* Word Bank				
account	bounce	growl	amount	without
frown	grouch	chowder	discount	prowl

/ou/ Spelled *ou*		

/ou/ Spelled *ow*		

Part 2: Select two of the words and use each in a sentence.

Word   **Sentence**

_____   _____

                    _____

_____   _____

Name _____   Date _____

Sentences and Suffixes

Part 1: Find a spelling word to complete each sentence.

1. The _____ on the clock has stopped swinging back and forth.

2. Our team was _____ with a score of 12-0.

3. The announcement was made before halftime _____ the game.

4. A decision about a new playground is _____ .

5. The necklace was gold with a ruby _____ .

6. The Fourth of July and Labor Day are two holidays that

    _____ during the summer.

7. The tail of one type of salamander is such an amazing _____ that it pops off if it is grabbed.

8. Fences _____ the gardens to keep rabbits and deer out.

Sentences and Suffixes

Part 2: The suffix *-ous* means full of or having. When adding *-ous* to base words that end in *y*, the *y* is changed to *i*. Add the suffix *-ous* to each word in the first column, write the word plus the suffix in the second column, and write its meaning in the third column.

Hint: Industry means steady effort and activity; working hard.

Base Word	Base Word + Suffix *-ous*	Meaning
1. glory		
2. vary		
3. victory		
4. mystery		
5. fury		
6. industry		

Name _____   Date _____

Solve the Quotable Quote

Find the correct word in the Spelling List that matches each clue. Transfer the numbered letters to the corresponding numbered spaces on the next page to uncover the quotable quote. When you complete the exercise, explain the meaning of the quote in your own words.

1. happen ___ ___ ___ ___
    5   2   12 14

2. 1/16 of a pound ___ ___ ___ ___ ___
                          6   9

3. tied up ___ ___ ___ ___ ___
                         13

4. permit ___ ___ ___ ___ ___
            1   11   16

5. sleepy ___ ___ ___ ___ ___ ___
                         7

6. the state north of Kansas ___ ___ ___ ___ ___ ___ ___ ___
                                                      10

7. angry ___ ___ ___ ___ ___ ___ ___
                    4

8. an arm or a leg ___ ___ ___ ___ ___ ___ ___ ___ ___
                     8

9. a locket or jewel that hangs from a necklace ___ ___ ___ ___ ___ ___ ___
                                                                          3

10. acting foolish, like a clown ___ ___ ___ ___ ___ ___ ___ ___ ___
                                                                    15

Solve the Quotable Quote

"   __ __ __ __ __ __ __   __ __ __ __ __
   1   2   3   4   5   6   7   7   8   9   1   10

  __ __ __ __ __ __   __ __ __ __
  11 5 12 13 9 14   3 15 1 6

  __ __ __ __ __ ."
  16 5 14 13 7

The quote means _____

_____

_____

Name _____ Date _____

Unit 28 Spelling List

Words that Follow the Rules

novice	(nov-ice)
apprentice	(ap-pren-tice)
service	(ser-vice)
notice	(no-tice)
justice	(jus-tice)
practice	(prac-tice)
furnace	(fur-nace)
palace	(pal-ace)
terrace	(ter-race)
menace	(men-ace)

Words with Suffixes: The suffix *-ous* means full of, having.

famous	(fame – e + ous)	(fam-ous)
ridiculous	(ridicule – e + ous)	(ri-dic-u-lous)
nervous	(nerve – e + ous)	(ner-vous)
desirous	(desire – e + ous)	(de-sir-ous)

Related Words

tent	(ten + t)	(tent)
tension	(ten + sion)	(ten-sion)
antenna	(an + ten + na)	(an-ten-na)
extend	(ex + ten + d)	(ex-tend)

Spelling Dangers

grief	(grief)
glacier	(gla-cier)

Proper Nouns

North Dakota	(North Da-ko-ta)
Utah	(U-tah)

Name _____ Date _____

Get to Know the States
North Dakota and Utah

Use the State Facts pages to complete Parts 1 and 2.

Part 1: Write the name of the state next to its capital.

	CAPITAL	STATE
1.	Bismarck	_____
2.	Salt Lake City	_____

Part 2: Write a sentence for each state that includes one fact about the state. Be sure to include the name of the state in your sentence.

1. _____

   _____

2. _____

   _____

Bonus: Tell the origin of the names Utah and North Dakota.

The name_____ comes from _____

_____.

The name _____ comes from _____

_____

Name _____   Date _____

Word Sort

Part 1: Sort the Words that Follow the Rules according to their spelling of /us/.

/us/ Spelled *ace*	

/us/ Spelled *ice*		

Part 2: Choose four of the words and use each in a sentence.

Word	Sentence
_____	_____
	_____
_____	_____
	_____
_____	_____
	_____
_____	_____
	_____

Name _____ Date _____

Sentences and Suffixes

Part 1: Find a spelling word to complete each sentence.

1. The _____ tore up trees and rocks as it moved down the mountain.

2. The big clown riding the tiny tricycle was a _____ sight.

3. When we go camping, we will sleep in a _____ .

4. The long _____ on the radio will help pick up the signal.

5. I am very _____ about performing before the group.

6. You could see the _____ on the little girl's face when she found out her kitten was lost.

7. My grandmother is _____ for her apple pies.

8. You could feel the _____ in the crowd as they waited for the player to take the free throw.

9. When the weather gets hot, I get _____ of a dip in the pool.

10. You will need to _____ the ladder all the way to reach to the second floor.

Sentences and Suffixes

Part 2: The suffix *-ous* means full of or having. When adding *-ous* to a base word that ends in *e*, drop the *e* before adding the suffix. Add the suffix *-ous* to each word in the first column, write the word plus the suffix in the second column, and write its meaning in the third column.

Base Word	Base Word + Suffix *-ous*	Meaning
1. fame		
2. desire		
3. ridicule		
4. nerve		

Name _____   Date _____

Crossword Fun

Use words from the Spelling List to solve the puzzle.

Crossword Fun

Across

2. the act of helping
6. to work at; to exercise or drill
10. royal residence, castle
11. an aerial or wire used for receiving radio signals
14. fairness, lawfulness
16. flat platform of earth with sloping sides
18. a beginner
19. a large body of ice moving down a slope
20. full of wants or wishes

Down

1. a danger, or a person who annoys
3. to stretch or make longer
4. a student learner
5. a boiler or heater
7. a shelter of canvas
8. full of anxiety
9. known by many people
12. an anxious feeling
13. absurd; being full of foolishness
15. to pay attention to
17. sadness

Name _____ Date _____

Unit 29 Spelling List

Words that Follow the Rules

doesn't	does not
won't	will not
there's	there is
who's	who is
shouldn't	should not
couldn't	could not
wouldn't	would not
let's	let us
they're	they are
you're	you are

Words with Suffixes: The suffix *-ship* means art or skill, or state of being.

leadership	(leader + ship)	(lead-er-ship)
friendship	(friend + ship)	(friend-ship)
horsemanship	(horseman + ship)	(horse-man-ship)
relationship	(relation + ship)	(re-la-tion-ship)

Related Words

elect	(e + lect)	(e-lect)
election	(e + lect + ion)	(e-lec-tion)
select	(se + lect)	(se-lect)
selection	(se + lect + ion)	(se-lec-tion)

Spelling Dangers

rehearsal	(re-hear-sal)
several	(sev-er-al)

Proper Nouns

Iowa	(I-o-wa)
Michigan	(Mich-i-gan)

Name _____   Date _____

Get to Know the States
Iowa and Michigan

Use the State Facts pages to complete Parts 1 and 2.

Part 1: Write the name of the state next to its capital.

            CAPITAL   STATE

    1. Lansing   _____

    2. Des Moines   _____

Part 2: Write a sentence for each state that includes one fact about the state. Be sure to include the name of the state in your sentence.

1. _____

   _____

2. _____

   _____

Bonus: Name the colors of the state flags of Iowa and Michigan.

The state flag of _____ is _____.

The state flag of _____ is _____

   _____.

Name _____   Date _____

Sentences and Suffixes

Part 1: Find a spelling word to complete each sentence.

1. In America, we _____ a president every four years.

2. The girls choir will have a _____ on Tuesday.

3. _____ go to the movies on Saturday.

4. _____ knocking on the door?

5. What flavor ice cream did you _____?

6. I will go to the show with you if _____ going.

7. The _____ of the town council will be held in November.

8. There are _____ people in front of me in line.

9. She _____ want to go with us.

10. It was difficult to make a _____ because we had so many choices.

11. Anne and I have known each other for many years and our

    _____ means so much to me.

12. _____ the book I was looking for!

13. The lid was stuck and I _____ open it.

14. Harry and Bob look so much alike that people think _____ twins.

Sentences and Suffixes

15. He _____ go to the movies with us because he doesn't like fantasy films.

16. Roberto is a good president; his _____ is important to our club.

17. We _____ cross the street in the middle of the block because it is dangerous.

18. Mom _____ let us walk to the library in the evening.

Part 2: The suffix -*ship* means art or skill, or state of being. Match the words with the suffix -*ship* to their meanings.

relationship	leadership	friendship
horsemanship	partnership	penmanship

1. the state of being friends _____

2. the art or skill of guiding people _____

3. skill in riding a horse _____

4. the art of writing with a pen _____

5. the state of being related or connected _____

6. the state of being a partner _____

Name _____   Date _____

Contraction Concentration

1. Cut the 20 game cards apart. Place them face down on the table.

2. Pick up two cards to see if they can be combined to form a contraction on the Spelling List. If they can, remove them from the space. If they cannot, return them face down to the space. Continue this process until all the cards are matched.

3. Write each pair of words and the contraction they make in the spaces below.

1. _____ + _____ = _____

2. _____ + _____ = _____

3. _____ + _____ = _____

4. _____ + _____ = _____

5. _____ + _____ = _____

6. _____ + _____ = _____

7. _____ + _____ = _____

8. _____ + _____ = _____

9. _____ + _____ = _____

10. _____ + _____ = _____

Contraction Concentration

does	is	would
are	there	not
should	us	could
not	who	not
you	is	will
not	they	are
let	not	

Name _____ Date _____

Unit 30 Spelling List

Words that Review Spelling Rules

autograph	(au-to-graph)
guessing	(guess-ing)
annoyed	(an-noyed)
poisonous	(poi-son-ous)
ounces	(oun-ces)
gown	(gown)
noticed	(no-ticed)
surface	(sur-face)
can't	cannot
here's	here is

Words that Review Suffixes

membership	(member + ship)	(mem-ber-ship)
weakness	(weak + ness)	(weak-ness)
adventurous	(adventure – e + ous)	(ad-ven-tur-ous)
continuous	(continue – e + ous)	(con-tin-u-ous)

Words that Review Related Words

formality	(form + ality)	(for-mal-i-ty)
auditions	(aud + itions)	(au-di-tions)
extending	(ex + ten + ding)	(ex-tend-ing)
elected	(e + lect + ed)	(e-lec-ted)

Name _____   Date _____

Get to Know the States Review

Write the name of the state next to its capital.

CAPITAL   STATE

1. Lansing   _____

2. Pierre   _____

3. Des Moines   _____

4. Salem   _____

5. Tallahassee   _____

6. Bismarck   _____

7. Lincoln   _____

8. Annapolis   _____

9. Salt Lake City   _____

10. Boise   _____

Bonus: Write the two-letter postal abbreviation after each state name. For example: New York NY

Name _____ Date _____

Spelling Rules and Suffixes

Part 1: Answer the questions with words from the Spelling List.

1. Which word has the /oi/ sound spelled *oi*? _____

2. Which word has the /f/ sound spelled *ph*? _____

3. Which words are contractions? _____

4. Which word has the /ou/ sound spelled *ou*? _____

5. Which word has the /ou/ sound spelled *ow*? _____

6. Which words contain the /us/ sound spelled *ice* or *ace*?

_____

7. Which word has the /g/ sound spelled *gu*? _____

8. Which word has the /oi/ sound spelled *oy*? _____

Spelling Rules and Suffixes

Part 2: Find the word in the Word Bank that answers the question. Write the word or words on the line and circle the suffix. Some words will be used for more than one answer.

Word Bank		
membership	adventurous	humorous
continuous	glorious	weakness

1. Which word has a suffix that means "the condition of being"?

   _____

2. In which word has the *y* of the base word been changed to *i* before the

   suffix was added? _____

3. What words have base words that did not change when their suffixes were added?

   _____

4. Which word has a suffix that means "condition or state"?

   _____

5. In what words has the final *e* of the base word been dropped before the

   suffix was added? _____

6. What words have a suffix that means "full of, having"?

   _____

   _____

Name _____   Date _____

Spelling Dangers

Find the words in the Spelling Dangers Word Bank that fit the clues.

Spelling Dangers Word Bank				
grief	occur	rehearsal	beauty	during
several	expect	opposite	glacier	favorite

1. has *dur* that sounds like *door* _____

2. has a silent *e* and an *o* that sounds like the *a* in *ago*

   _____   _____

3. has *ie* that sounds like long *e* _____

4. has a silent *a* and *al* that sounds like /ul/ _____

5. has a *y* that sounds like long *e* and an *a* that is silent

   _____

6. has *al* that sounds like /ul/ and an *e* that can be silent or pronounced like the

   a in *ago* _____

7. has a /sh/ sound spelled *ci* _____

8. has an *x* that sounds like /ks/ _____

9. has an *o* that sounds like the *a* in ago and /k/ sound spelled *cc*

   _____

Name _____   Date _____

It's All the Same

Find a spelling word that means the same or almost the same as the underlined word or words in each sentence.

1. The president of the club was <u>chosen by vote</u> yesterday.

   _____

2. I <u>saw</u> that the toy store is having a sale. _____

3. We are <u>lengthening</u> our vacation by two days. _____

4. The older dog seemed <u>bothered</u> by the puppy. _____

5. The <u>top</u> of the table was smooth and shiny. _____

6. I hope to get the batter to <u>write his name on</u> the ball he hit into the stands.

   _____

7. Some types of mushrooms are <u>capable of harming or killing</u> if eaten.

   _____

8. The fairy godmother turned Cinderella's rags into a beautiful <u>dress</u>.

   _____

9. The <u>daring</u> explorers set off into the unexplored jungle.

   _____

10. The links were joined to make one <u>endless</u> loop.

It's All the Same

11. I'm <u>supposing</u> that you'd like to go to the movies with us.

   _____

12. <u>Here is</u> the book I need. _____

13. The lack of food and water caused the shipwrecked sailor's <u>condition of</u>

   <u>lacking strength.</u> _____

14. The <u>short performances to test the talents</u> for singers will be held next week.

   _____

15. The container held six <u>units of weight equal to 1/16 of a pound</u>.

   _____

16. The <u>condition of being a member</u> in the club is open to all boys and girls 10

   and older. _____

17. I <u>cannot</u> lift the package. _____

18. Many people e-mail invitations rather than bother with the <u>state of being</u>

   <u>formal</u> of handwriting them. _____

Name   Date

Unit 31 Spelling List

Words that Follow the Rules

windshield	(wind-shield)
masterpiece	(mas-ter-piece)
supermarket	(su-per-mar-ket)
wristwatch	(wrist-watch)
background	(back-ground)
anywhere	(an-y-where)
campground	(camp-ground)
earthquake	(earth-quake)
handshake	(hand-shake)
overlook	(o-ver-look)

Words with Suffixes: The suffix *-ology* means the study of.

musicology	(music + ology)	(mu-si-col-o-gy)
biology	(bi + ology)	(bi-ol-o-gy)
zoology	(zo + ology)	(zo-ol-o-gy)
geology	(ge + ology)	(ge-ol-o-gy)

Related Words

vitamin	(vita + min)	(vi-ta-min)
vital	(vita + l)	(vi-tal)
vitality	(vita + lity)	(vi-tal-i-ty)
revitalize	(re + vita + lize)	(re-vi-tal-ize)

Spelling Dangers

scissors	(scis-sors)
necessary	(nec-es-sar-y)

Proper Nouns

United States	(U-nit-ed States)
Washington, D.C.	(Wash-ing-ton, D.C.)

Name _____   Date _____

Get to Know the United States and Washington, D.C.

Facts about the United States
- Made up of 50 states and the District of Columbia (Washington, D.C.)
- National bird: bald eagle
- National motto: "E Pluribus Unum" "One from Many"
- National anthem: "The Star Spangled Banner"

Facts about Washington, D.C.
- Capital of the United States
- Washington is named for the first president, George Washington; District of Columbia is named for Christopher Columbus
- Motto: "Justice for all"
- Bird: wood thrush
- Flower: American beauty rose

Part 1: Write the name of the country and its capital.

COUNTRY   CAPITAL

_____   _____

Part 2: Write a sentence about the United States and one about Washington, D.C., and include one fact in each sentence. Be sure to include the names United States and Washington, D.C., in your sentences.

1.

_____

_____

2.

_____

_____

Bonus: On the back of this page, describe the United States flag and the flag of Washington, D.C. Be sure to include the names of the city and the country in your sentences.

Name _____   Date _____

Sentences and Suffixes

Part 1: Complete each sentence with a spelling word.

1. In the painting there were mountains in the _____ and a village in the foreground.

2. When something is required, that means it is _____ .

3. A _____ is used as a greeting or a farewell.

4. We can go _____ you'd like to go on Saturday.

5. We drink milk which contains _____ D to give us healthy bones.

6. If you build something without first reading the directions, you might

   _____ an important step.

7. I want to learn more about animals so I will take a _____ course in college.

8. Dad hopes a new coat of paint will _____ the family room.

9. Food and water are _____ to life.

10. Please bring the _____ so I can cut the paper.

11. The little old man had so much _____ , he seemed to skip rather than walk.

12. When we drove into the mud, it splashed up and covered the

    _____ .

Sentences and Suffixes

Part 2: The suffix *-ology* means the study of. Match the words with the suffix *-ology* with their meanings.

geology	mythology	biology
musicology	zoology	audiology

Hint: Remember that the root *aud* means to hear.

1. the study of music _____

2. the study of plants and animals (living things) _____

3. the study of hearing _____

4. the study of the history of the earth as recorded in rocks

    _____

5. the study of myths _____

6. the study of animals _____

Name _____ Date _____

One of the Group

Write the spelling word that belongs in each group.

1. sculpture, statue, tapestry, _____

2. tires, steering wheel, seats, _____

3. campfires, tents, campers, _____

4. grandfather clock, sundial, cuckoo clock, _____

5. sword, knife, shears, _____

6. lights, costumes, props, _____

7. hardware store, toy store, department store, _____

8. mountain top, top of a tower, top of a building, _____

9. flood, hurricane, tornado, _____

10. England, Japan, Canada, _____

Name   Date

Unit 32 Spelling List

Words that Follow the Rules

tail	(tail)
tale	(tale)
mail	(mail)
male	(male)
groan	(groan)
grown	(grown)
waist	(waist)
waste	(waste)
berry	(ber-ry)
bury	(bur-y)

Words with Suffixes: The suffix -*ive* means full of, or tending toward.

active	(act + ive)	(act-ive)
instructive	(instruct + ive)	(in-struct-ive)
protective	(protect + ive)	(pro-tect-ive)
destructive	(destruct + ive)	(de-struct-ive)

Related Words

century	(cent + ury)	(cen-tu-ry)
cent	(cent)	(cent)
percent	(per + cent)	(per-cent)
centipede	(cent + ipede)	(cen-ti-pede)

Spelling Dangers

experience	(ex-pe-ri-ence)
existence	(ex-ist-ence)

Proper Nouns

Canada	(Can-a-da)
Mexico	(Mex-i-co)

Name _____   Date _____

Get to Know Canada and Mexico

Facts about Canada
- Located to the north of the United States
- Capital city: Ottawa
- Major languages spoken: English and French
- National symbol: maple leaf

Facts about Mexico
- Located to the south of the United States
- Capital city: Mexico City
- Official name: United Mexican States
- Major language spoken: Spanish

Part 1: Write the name of the country next to its capital.

CAPITAL   COUNTRY

1. Mexico City   _____

2. Ottawa   _____

Part 2: Write a sentence about Canada and one about Mexico and include one fact about the country in each sentence. Be sure to include the names of the countries in your sentences.

1. _____

   _____

2. _____

   _____

Bonus: On the back of this page, write a sentence that tells the name of the body of water that forms the western border of Canada and Mexico. Be sure to include the names of the countries in your sentence.

_____

Name _____   Date _____

Definitions and Suffixes

Part 1: Find a spelling word that matches each definition.

1. one hundred years   _____

2. to place in the ground and cover   _____

3. the state of being alive   _____

4. material that is thrown away   _____

5. a penny   _____

6. tending toward protection or safety   _____

7. to have become larger or increased   _____

8. wormlike animal with many pairs of legs   _____

9. a story   _____

10. a man or a boy   _____

11. a hundredth part   _____

12. a deep sound that shows sorrow, pain,   _____
    annoyance, or disapproval

13. small fruit   _____

14. the rear part of an animal   _____

15. something carried in the postal system   _____

Definitions and Suffixes

Part 2: The suffix -ive means full of, or tending toward. Match the words with the suffix -ive to their meanings.

instructive	destructive	attractive
constructive	active	protective

1. tending toward protection or safety _____

2. tending toward or full of action and movement _____

3. full of attraction _____

4. tending toward destruction or breaking up, tearing down, or ruining

   _____

5. tending toward construction or building up _____

6. full of material for instruction _____

Name _____ Date _____

Homophone Hunt

Circle the homophone that belongs in each sentence.

1. Please check to see if there is a letter for me in today's (male, mail).

2. My dog will (bury, berry) his bone in the yard.

3. The squirrel has a bushy (tail, tale).

4. The girl had a blue sash around her (waste, waist).

5. The fairy (tale, tail) had a happy ending.

6. Wheat and corn are (groan, grown) in the central part of the United States.

7. The (male, mail) lion has a mane, but the female doesn't.

8. The bird ate the red (berry, bury) on the bush.

9. Don't (waste, waist) the glue; use only a small amount.

10. Dad's jokes sometimes make me (groan, grown).

Name _____   Date _____

Unit 33 Spelling List

Words that Follow the Rules
close	(close)
clothes	(clothes)
deer	(deer)
dear	(dear)
hour	(hour)
our	(our)
hear	(hear)
here	(here)
heard	(heard)
herd	(herd)

Words with Suffixes: The suffix *-ment* changes a verb to a noun.
punishment	(punish + ment)	(pun-ish-ment)
reinforcement	(reinforce + ment)	(re-in-force-ment)
treatment	(treat + ment)	(treat-ment)
enrollment	(enroll + ment)	(en-roll-ment)

Related Words
circus	(circ + us)	(cir-cus)
circle	(circ + le)	(cir-cle)
circular	(circ + ular)	(cir-cu-lar)
circulation	(circ + ulation)	(cir-cu-la-tion)

Spelling Dangers
humorous	(hu-mor-ous)
beautiful	(beau-ti-ful)

Proper Nouns
America	(A-mer-i-ca)
Africa	(Af-ri-ca)

Name _____   Date _____

Get to Know Africa and (North and South) America

Facts about Africa
- Second-largest continent
- Longest river – Nile
- Largest country – Sudan

Facts about South America
- Fourth-largest continent
- Longest river – Amazon
- Largest country – Brazil

Facts about North America
- Third-largest continent
- Longest river – Mississippi
- Largest country – Canada

Part 1: Write the continents in order according to their sizes (beginning with the largest).

1. _____

2. _____

3. _____

Part 2: Write sentences about any two of the continents listed above. In each sentence include one fact about the continent and the continent's name.

1. _____

_____

2. _____

_____

Bonus: On the back of this page, write three sentences that tell the directions you would have to travel to get from Africa to North America, from North America to South America, and from South America to Africa. Be sure to include the names of the continents in your sentences.

Name _____ Date _____

Give Me a Clue

Find a spelling word to match each clue.

1. If you do something wrong, you might receive this. _____

2. This has no beginning and no end. _____

3. You might find this animal in a meadow or forest. _____

4. This describes the shape of a roll of tape. _____

5. This means something belongs to us. _____

6. This is the movement of blood through veins and arteries. _____

7. This kind of story will make you laugh. _____

8. If your dog has fleas he might need this to get rid of them. _____

9. A group of cattle, buffalo, or deer is called this. _____

10. You wear these. _____

11. You can see clowns and trained animals here. _____

12. A garden could be described this way and so could a person or an artwork. _____

13. A sagging shelf might need this. _____

14. If your name is on this, it is on the list. _____

15. Come to this place instead of going there. _____

Name _____ Date _____

Homophone Bingo

Your teacher will read sentences that contain homophones from Units 32 and 33. Listen to each sentence and find the homophone that matches on your card. Spell it aloud. If your answer is correct, cover the word with a marker. If your answer is incorrect, try again with the next sentence. You can have bingo horizontally, vertically, diagonally, and four corners.

Homophone Bingo			
our	grown	close	hour
waste	herd	berry	dear
clothes	bury	hear	heard
here	deer	groan	waist

Homophone Bingo

Homophone Bingo			

Name _____   Date _____

Synonyms and Suffixes

Part 1: Find a spelling word that means the same or almost the same as the word or words below. You may use a dictionary or thesaurus.

1. listen _____

2. shut _____

3. precious _____

4. round _____

5. lovely _____

6. funny _____

7. garment or apparel _____

8. registration _____

9. drive _____

10. sixty minutes _____

Synonyms and Suffixes

Part 2: The suffix *-ment* changes a verb to a noun. Add the suffix *-ment* to the verbs listed, then select three of the nouns and use each in a sentence.

Verb	Verb + Suffix *-ment* = Noun
1. enroll	
2. disagree	
3. reinforce	
4. treat	
5. replace	
6. punish	

1. _____

   _____

   _____

2. _____

   _____

   _____

3. _____

   _____

   _____

Name _____   Date _____

Unit 34 Spelling List

Words that Follow the Rules

presence   (pres-ence)
presents   (pres-ents)
pause   (pause)
paws   (paws)
chews   (chews)
choose   (choose)
rose   (rose)
rows   (rows)
days   (days)
daze   (daze)

Words with Suffixes: The suffix *-ful* means full of, having.

fearful   (fear + ful)   (fear-ful)
painful   (pain + ful)   (pain-ful)
truthful   (truth + ful)   (truth-ful)
successful   (success + ful)   (suc-cess-ful)

Related Words

divide   (divi + de)   (di-vide)
division   (divi + sion)   (di-vi-sion)
individual   (in + divi + dual) (in-di-vid-u-al)
indivisible   (in + divi + sible) (in-di-vis-i-ble)

Spelling Dangers

measure   (meas-ure)
pleasant   (pleas-ant)

Proper Nouns

Asia   (A-sia)
Europe   (Eu-rope)

Name _____   Date _____

Get to Know Europe and Asia

Facts about Europe
- Second-smallest continent
- Largest city – Moscow
- Longest river – Volga
- Tallest mountains – Alps

Facts about Asia
- Largest continent
- Largest city – Tokyo
- Longest river – Chang Jiang (Yangtze)
- Tallest mountains – Himalayas

Part 1: Write the continents in order according to their size, larger to smaller.

    1. _____

    2. _____

Part 2: Write a sentence for each continent that includes one fact about the continent. Be sure to include the names of the continents in your sentences.

1. _____

   _____

2. _____

   _____

Bonus: On the back of this page, write a sentence that tells the name of the mountain range that forms a natural border between Europe and Asia. Be sure to include the names of the continents in your sentence.

Name _____   Date _____

Definitions and the Suffix *-ful*

Part 1: Find a spelling word that matches each definition.

1. to select _____

2. gifts _____

3. feet of a four-footed animal _____

4. horizontal lines of seats _____

5. 24-hour periods that begin at midnight _____

6. fact of being present _____

7. to stun or make dizzy _____

8. brief stop _____

9. past of rise _____

10. grinds with the teeth _____

Definitions and the Suffix *-ful*

Part 2: The suffix *-ful* means full of, having. Match the words with the suffix *-ful* to their meanings.

truthful	fearful	harmful
joyful	painful	successful

1. full of pain, suffering _____

2. having success; having gained wealth or fame _____

3. full of joy; happy _____

4. having the quality of honesty (telling the truth) _____

5. full of harm; likely to cause hurt or damage _____

6. full of fear or causing fear _____

Name _____   Date _____

It's All the Same

Find a spelling word that means the same or almost the same as the underlined word or words in each sentence. You may use a dictionary or thesaurus.

1. "The Pledge of Allegiance" describes America as a nation that is <u>not able to</u>

   <u>be separated</u>. _____

2. When we heard the storm approaching, we were <u>afraid</u>.

   _____

3. The <u>thriving</u> business employs many workers. _____

4. <u>Separate</u> the cupcakes among the guests. _____

5. The flowers in the garden have a <u>nice</u> smell. _____

6. Dad will <u>gauge</u> the size of the room before buying a new rug.

   _____

7. The boy's unkind words were <u>hurtful</u> to the girl. _____

8. The <u>person</u> met me at the movies at the mall. _____

9. The answer given by the witness was <u>honest</u>. _____

10. He made an equal <u>separation</u> of blocks among the four children.

    _____

Name _____ Date _____

Unit 35 Spelling List

Words that Follow the Rules

mist	(mist)
missed	(missed)
guest	(guest)
guessed	(guessed)
find	(find)
fined	(fined)
toad	(toad)
towed	(towed)
aloud	(a-loud)
allowed	(al-lowed)

Words with Suffixes: The suffix *-ic* means having characteristics of, relating to.

angelic	(angel + ic)	(an-gel-ic)
artistic	(artist + ic)	(ar-tist-ic)
aquatic	(aquat + ic)	(a-quat-ic)
graphic	(graph + ic)	(graph-ic)

Related Words

image	(imag + e)	(im-age)
imagine	(imag + ine)	(i-mag-ine)
imaginary	(imag + inary)	(i-mag-i-nar-y)
imagination	(imag + ination)	(i-mag-i-na-tion)

Spelling Dangers

Wednesday	(Wednes-day)
Tuesday	(Tues-day)

Proper Nouns

Australia	(Aus-tral-ia)
Antarctica	(Ant-arc-ti-ca)

Name _____ Date _____

Get to Know Australia and Antarctica

Facts about Australia
- Smallest continent
- Island, bordered by Pacific and Indian oceans
- Called the "Land Down Under"
- Home to the kangaroo, wallaby, and platypus

Facts about Antarctica
- Fifth-largest continent
- Island, bordered by the Atlantic, Pacific, and Indian oceans
- Coldest and windiest place on Earth
- Home to seals, penguins, and whales

Part 1: Write the continents in order according to their size, larger to smaller.

1. _____

2. _____

Part 2: Write a sentence for each continent that includes one fact about the continent. Be sure to include the names of the continents in your sentences.

1. _____

_____

2. _____

_____

Bonus: On the back of this page, write a sentence describing where in the world Australia and Antarctica are located. Be sure to include the names of the continents in your sentence.

Name _____   Date _____

Homophone Hunt and the Suffix *-ic*

Part 1: Circle the homophone that belongs in each sentence.

1. I wasn't sure so I (guessed, guest) the answer.

2. My dad's car broke down and had to be (toad, towed).

3. He is not (allowed, aloud) to go to the game.

4. I was (fined, find) because the book was overdue.

5. The (toad, towed) has bumpy skin.

6. The rain fell as a fine (missed, mist).

7. When did you (fined, find) the missing glove?

8. I am bringing my cousin to the pool as my (guessed, guest).

9. My sister and I like to read (allowed, aloud) to each other.

10. We (missed, mist) the exit on the highway and had to go back.

Homophone Hunt and the Suffix -ic

Part 2: The suffix -ic means having characteristics of, relating to. Match the words with the suffix -ic to their meanings.

aquatic	angelic	artistic
historic	graphic	poetic

1. relating to the water _____

2. having characteristics of an angel; good, beautiful, helpful

   _____

3. relating to pictures, etching, engraving _____

4. relating to history _____

5. relating to or having characteristics of poets or poetry

   _____

6. relating to the arts or having characteristics of an artist

   _____

Name _____ Date _____

Synonyms and Sentences

Part 1: Find a spelling word that means the same or almost the same as the words below.

1. permitted   _____

2. discover   _____

3. visitor   _____

4. haze   _____

5. imagined   _____

6. overlooked   _____

7. charged   _____

8. pulled   _____

Part 2: Find a spelling word to complete each sentence.

1. The child made up a story about an _____ animal.

2. People say that my sister is very _____ because she draws and paints well.

3. The author who writes stories about a talking dog has a great

   _____.

4. The swimmers practiced at the _____ center.

Synonyms and Sentences

5. The little boy was very sweet and had an _____ smile.

6. When I am reading a book, I try to _____ how the characters look and sound.

7. My aunt, who is a _____ artist, takes photographs and does etching.

8. My pet _____ is fat-bodied and slow, while my frog is slim and speedy.

9. Whose _____ is on the dollar bill?

10. If you start the week with Monday, the next two days are

    _____ and _____.

Name   Date

Unit 36 Spelling List

Words that Review Spelling Rules

someone	(some-one)
headache	(head-ache)
so	(so)
sew	(sew)
sow	(sow)
road	(road)
rowed	(rowed)
rode	(rode)
lesson	(les-son)
lessen	(les-sen)

Words that Review Suffixes

scientific	(scientif + ic)	(sci-en-tif-ic)
wonderful	(wonder + ful)	(won-der-ful)
enjoyment	(enjoy + ment)	(en-joy-ment)
corrective	(correct + ive)	(cor-rec-tive)

Words that Review Related Words

images	(imag + es)	(im-ag-es)
divided	(divi + ded)	(di-vid-ed)
centuries	(cent + uries)	(cen-tu-ries)
vitamins	(vita + mins)	(vi-ta-mins)

Name _____   Date _____

Get to Know the World Review

Put the continents Africa, North America, South America, Europe, Asia, Antarctica, and Australia, in order according to size (largest to smallest). Then do the same for the countries Canada, Mexico, and the United States, and Washington, D.C.

Hint: The United States is larger than Mexico.

Continents

1. _____

2. _____

3. _____

4. _____

5. _____

6. _____

7. _____

Countries and Washington, D.C.

1. _____

2. _____

3. _____

4. _____

Bonus: On the back of this page, tell which of the parts of the world listed above the equator passes through.

Name _____   Date _____

Spelling Rules and Suffixes

Part 1: Answer the questions with words from the Spelling List.

1. Which two words are compound words? _____

   _____

2. Which two words are plurals that were formed by adding -s to the base word?

   _____   _____

3. Which word is a plural formed by changing the y of the base word to i and

   adding -es? _____

4. Which two homophones are verbs in the past tense?

   _____   _____

5. Which six words contain the sound of long o? _____

   _____   _____

   _____   _____

   _____

6. Which pair of homophones have the sound of /en/?

   _____   _____

Spelling Rules and Suffixes

Part 2: Find the word in the Word Bank that answers the question. Write the word or words on the line and circle the suffix. Some words will be used for more than one answer.

Word Bank		
effective	wonderful	corrective
meteorology	enjoyment	scientific

1. Which word has a suffix that means "full of"? _____

2. Which word has a suffix that means "relating to" or "having characteristics of"?

   _____

3. Which word has a suffix that changes a verb to a noun?

   _____

4. Which word has a suffix that means "the study of"? _____

5. Which words are nouns? _____

6. Which words have a suffix that means "full of" or "tending toward"?

   _____   _____

Name _____   Date _____

Spelling Dangers

Find the words in the Spelling Dangers Word Bank that fit the clues.

Spelling Dangers Word Bank				
pleasant	beautiful	experience	measure	Tuesday
necessary	scissors	Wednesday	humorous	existence

1. *c* sounds like /s/ and *y* sounds like long *e* _____

2. *ea* sounds like short *e* and *sure* sounds like /sher/ or /zher/

   _____

3. has a silent *d* and ends in the sound of long *a* _____

4. has a silent *a* and a suffix that means "full of" _____

5. *ex* sounds like /ik/, *c* sounds like /s/, and *i* sounds like long *e*

   _____

6. *ea* sounds like short *e* and *ant* sounds like /ent/ _____

7. double *s* and final *s* sound like /z/, and *or* sounds like /er/

   _____

8. has a short *i*, *ex* sounds like /ik/, and *c* sounds like /s/

   _____

9. *or* sounds like /er/ and *ous* sounds like /us/ _____

10. first syllable sounds like /tooz/ _____

Name _____   Date _____

Crossword Fun

Crossword Fun

Across

1. past tense of row
2. in order that
4. separated into parts
8. pictures
9. full of wonder; something that causes amazement
10. tending toward correcting
12. relating to science
13. street or path
16. pleasure
17. a pain in the head

Down

1. past tense of ride
3. an exercise for a student to learn
5. substances found in natural foods that are needed for good health
6. a person
7. use a needle and thread to fasten stitches
11. hundreds of years
14. to make less
15. to scatter or spread